IN SEARCH
of
CHRISTIANITY

Edited by Tony Moss

Foreword by Dr Robert Runcie
Archbishop of Canterbury

Firethorn Press

Firethorn Press is an imprint of Waterstone & Co. Limited

First published 1986
by
Waterstone & Co. Limited
49 Hay's Mews
London W1X 7RT

Typeset by Cambrian Typesetters,
Frimley, Camberley, Surrey.
Printed and bound in Great Britain by
Richard Clay PLC, Bungay, Suffolk.

IN SEARCH
of
CHRISTIANITY

Foreword from the Archbishop of Canterbury

These essays do much to correct the fashionable media image of the Church of England as confused, divided and marginal. They also call into question the gloomy assumption that secularism has already advanced irresistibly and irreversibly. Instead, each contributor shows – with a bracing mixture of clarity, realism and vigour – how far our Church-men and women are already recovering a strong sense of credal direction and responsibility for the future. I welcome this collection as an important contribution both to current debate and to a proper Christian confidence.

CONTENTS

INTRODUCTION

Defending Christianity on British television has not proved to be the happiest of experiences in recent years. An increasingly sceptical world at large has been only too quick to focus on anything which smacks of irrational mumbo-jumbo while the self-proclaimed guardians of the faith have been even quicker to jump on anyone who professes a hint of uncertainty or doubt.

This has undoubtedly been the experience of many of those contributing to this collection when appearing on London Weekend Television's CREDO programme. This is, in fact, hardly surprising as CREDO has adopted a unique approach to religion, treating it as a subject which demands critical investigation and analysis. Our investigations have often focused on Christianity, examining how Church leaders have been wrestling with the problems of expressing their faith in a scientific and secular age.

In pursuing this approach CREDO has brought to light major conflicts within the Christian world over the nature of that faith, the character of God and the importance of the bible. The effect has been dramatic — the popular press predicting the end of Christianity as we know it and protestors calling for doubting Bishops to be denounced, defrocked or decapitated.

It is richly ironic that many of those protests have come from quarters where absolutely no credence is given to the very beliefs over which Church leaders have been hesitating. This was perfectly illustrated by a newspaper editorial which stated, "Whatever one thinks of Christianity (i.e. not very much) it is quite clear what it stands for, and any Church leader who doubts this has no alternative but to resign."

In reality, many of the controversies which seem to have surfaced recently are not new. Throughout Christian history, theologians have struggled to reconcile the doctrines of the Church with their own perceptions of the world about them.

Indeed it is not just intellectuals who have questioned the doctrines. Ordinary believers have, from the first century, found it hard to accept the "resurrection of the body" found in the creeds, being aware of the inevitable process of bodily degeneration.

Despite this, it is true that the divisions within Christianity today are serious and undoubtedly getting greater all the time. "In Search of Christianity" contains a range of essays which try to assess the state of this current conflict and look at what might happen to the Christian religion in the future.

The main thrust of this collection, however, is to give leading Christian figures an opportunity to articulate their vision of Christianity and describe what it means to believe in the God of Jesus Christ.

What emerges is a surprisingly coherent expression of faith, phrased in ways which illustrate a determination to engage with the doubts and objections of a rational culture.

This is in essence what makes it possible for CREDO and individual people to undertake a serious search into Christianity. For there are many religious cults on the ascendancy today, with the strangest amalgam of unlikely beliefs, which rely on uncritical acceptance as the first price to pay on the toll road to the inner sanctum. A debate over questions of truth is never on the agenda.

The British Israel movement, for example, believes that the white man of Britain is the true – and only true – descendant of the ten lost tribes of Israel and the legitimate heir to the promises made by God to Abraham. It is he alone who will inherit the Kingdom of heaven. The rest be damned.

This may seem unfair, implausible or even downright ridiculous but that is what they believe and there is no scope for a rational discussion.

Similarly, many astrologers are wedded to the belief that individual destiny is shaped by the conjunction of planets at birth and count as significant only those planets which had been discovered 3,000 years ago when the astrological world was founded.

Christian thinkers have always wanted to question beliefs which face such a staggering array of scientific, philosophical and moral problems. This collection illustrates that Christianity responds and reacts to commonsense and rational questioning in a way which few religious systems would ever consider.

But while reason has its place, the heart of Christian belief lies beyond – in professing a faith in something which is greater than human comprehension. It is a religion which says there is reason to believe and in faith that belief may be enriched by experience. Experience of God.

During the making of numerous CREDO television programmes I have met in many Christians a quality which does suggest they experience what may be a genuine glimpse of the source of our being: I sense amid all the current controversy a hint of a truth drawing the intelligent enquires further into a search for Christianity.

Tony Moss, December 1985
Associate Producer, LWT's CREDO

Christianity in Crisis

Tony Moss

July 1984. Flames leapt into the dark night. York Minster was burning. Fire remorselessly ate into the priceless tapestries and destroyed the ancient stained-glass. Eyewitnesses who saw the blaze begin claim they saw bolts of lightning strike the Minster spire and heard a great crack echo from the building.

This fire provoked an immediate controversy mirroring many of the furious rows which had been a feature of Christian circles for months. Some said the Minster fire had been poetic justice, others claimed it was more than that. For just two days before, the Minster had hosted the consecration of the controversial new Bishop of Durham, amid anger and recriminations.

Dr David Jenkins had infuriated many traditionalists within the Church by publicly dismissing certain key aspects of the Christian faith, notably that Jesus was born of a virgin and rose from the dead. His enthronement service had been picketed and interrupted with abusive heckling.

Many people saw the attack of lightning as a divine warning of anger against the Bishop's heresy and the general heretical direction of the Church of England. (They refused to speculate on why lightning had also struck three other churches on the same night; churches which had no connection with David Jenkins). The leadership of the Church, of course, saw things rather differently. The Archbishop of Canterbury, Dr Robert Runcie, claimed it was a miracle that the Minster had not been completely gutted and thanked God for giving strength and courage to the firemen who had controlled the blaze.

By contrast, the Archbishop of York, Dr John Habgood, refuted all suggestions that God had sent down the lightning or helped to save the Minster. He stated that God did not intervene in that sort of manner at all.

The controversy surrounding the fire was just the culmination of a sequence of heated arguments which, in the space of a few months, brought all the deepest disputes within the Christian world out into the public gaze; not to mention the gaze of the Church's own believers, from whom it had been sheltered for years.

Disputes within university theology and history departments, disputes in theological training colleges, disputes bubbling under the surface of the Church's Synod and even disputes which had wracked the Catholic Church throughout the world – all began to spill out through the pulpits, newspapers and most dramatically on television.

While David Jenkins became the touchstone for many of the emerging disputes, his thoughts on the virgin birth and the resurrection were in many ways the result of certain earlier debates rather than the source of fresh and original ones. For during the past decade Christian thinkers have undertaken a plethora of debates, radically questioning the nature of God and Christian faith in the light of many forces from positivist philosophy, scientific understanding, humanitarian values and basic commonsense. Is it still possible to believe in God, Jesus Christ, life after death, heaven and hell, miracles or divine providence? Does God really answer prayer? Do all non-Christians face eternal damnation? Is sex before marriage a mortal sin? What about homosexuality? How true is the bible? Are women inferior to men? What about the Ten Commandments?

And so it goes on. Beliefs about the nature of Christianity and what it has to say about modern living were all being questioned within intellectual circles by Christians who could no longer assent to the old certainties in the face of so many objections from the outside world.

The liveliest and most searching debate centred on the very heart of Christianity: belief in God. Very soon a group of priests and theologians left the mainstream faith far behind, pronouncing that their deliberations had forced them to conclude that 'God is Dead.' They argued that rational man must accept that nothing exists beyond his grasp and that nothing is possible beyond what science can predict. The miraculous events in the bible were either fraudulent or had a rational explanation. God was an invention of primitive, pre-scientific man and was himself a fraud.

People do frequently lose their faith in a religion, stop believing in its dogma and become avowed atheists. But several of those who had come to these conclusions argued that they were still Christians in the true sense of the word but were expressing their Christianity in modern language. Don Cupitt, a Cambridge priest and academic, has argued this most persuasively, and refused to give up his Anglican cloth. He says that pre-scientific, pre-rational people had invented the name 'God' as a way of making sense of their lives – and that Christianity today should proclaim this truth without holding on to the primitive idea of a supernatural being. "I do believe in God in that when we speak of God, we speak of the guiding spirit of our lives – that which we make sacred. Our spiritual and moral aims and values, that is our true God and it is a God which lives within, not an external, objective reality."

Very few Christians adopted this course of action – giving up faith in God while continuing to claim oneself a Christian – but the intellectual questions raised by Cupitt and others remained important for an increasing number of theologians and Church leaders. As time wore on, pressures within the Church of England grew to address some of these questions.

It was the Church of England which proved to be the only Christian body that seriously attempted to tackle any of the questions – for two reasons. The C of E was proud of its composition as a "broad church" including enormous doctrinal differences within its embrace. While that other great "broad church", the Labour Party, has invariably seen its broadness as a basis for constant internal dispute, the C of E has seen it as a very sound reason for avoiding doctrinal disputes at all costs. Yet the very role of the Church of England as a national institution, reflecting and representing the national religious ethos and upholding Christian moral standards, made it inevitable that it would have to respond to secular pressures and intellectual ideas.

The Church has always had a close link with the Establishment and the prevailing philosophies of the time and could not ignore the influence of science and rationalism forever. It was the very broadness of the Anglican church's membership which brought about the need for some thought about what Christian faith means in the twentieth century. Many clergymen were infuriated by the refusal of priests like Don Cupitt to renounce their ordained ministry. And trends within the Church strengthened the critics of the Cupitts.

The evangelical wing of the Church has been growing for at least a decade, recruiting amongst the young and students in particular; but it found its confidence and its voice only as the extreme liberals veered off the map of established Christianity. For in the seventies the liberals still held sway as leading Churchmen prepared to open up debate about Christian essentials.

The first move was a 1976 Doctrine Commission report entitled "The Nature of Christian Faith and Its Expression in Holy Scripture and the Creeds". Although it was an impressive document there was not yet sufficient pressure within the Church for a real debate over fundamentals, and the document, undiscussed, collected the dust in Lambeth Palace.

When the liberal Bishop of Winchester, John Taylor, became chairman of the Doctrine Commission in the early eighties, many expected the debate proper would begin. For in his radical work, "The Go-Between God", he argued for a fundamental rethinking of the nature of God.

The traditional picture of God has relied heavily on a notion of an all-powerful creator who controlled the universe in every last detail. Up until the Enlightenment people often attributed every event in the world from rainfall to harvests on the immediate will of God to reward or punish individuals for their behaviour. Science inevitably modified this perception but Christians continued to believe that God is ultimately behind it all, organising the operation of the universe and exacting justice.

The moral implications of this have always been frightening. Earthquakes, infant mortality, genocide – few Christians could ever detect God at work here; yet if God really controlled the world then such consequences appear to follow. John Taylor suggested that rethinking about God had to begin with the question of his power. He argued that God was not in ultimate control of the universe; he created the universe but in doing so created a variety of forces over whose potential direction he would not maintain control. By relinquishing his power he was freely giving the universe the chance to develop – and with the emergence of conscious man, to determine the course of history. Taylor claimed that God did not intervene arbitrarily throughout history but restricted himself to working through individuals who invited his love to blossom in their lives.

John Drury, Dean of King's College, Cambridge saw these thoughts as a great break with previous ways of understanding God. "God's power had always been seen as despotic or autocratic whereas now we're talking about a loving influence which works only through persuasion – human beings have to accept ultimate responsibility for their actions."

In this light, God is seen not as causing human suffering but sharing in it as part of the forces which are at work through human life. This train of thought raises the possibility that God, no longer all-powerful, may have to witness mankind destroying his creation; a possibility which John Taylor recognises, "I believe that God is at risk and the consequences are not certain. We could overturn the whole thing but God would still be there, starting again."

Taylor was primarily addressing questions of morality in thinking about the character of God, attempting to reconcile the suffering and injustice in the world with the idea of a loving God. His ideas were not popular with many traditionalists, for in solving some problems Taylor's conception of God raised far more – how does one understand God's miraculous interventions, supremely the intervention of Jesus, if not as an all-powerful creator breaking in to direct the world in his light? How can a loving God choose to leave the destiny of his creation to its own whims? And so on.

From the perspective of a sceptical rationalist, the Taylor understanding of God emerges as no more plausible than the old man in the sky. Overall, this thinking produced few ripples but even less confidence within the Church.

The moral character of Christianity was next brought into question with the publication of the Church's report on "Inter-Faith Dialogue" which considered what attitudes the

Church should adopt to other religions. Traditionally, the Christian Church was adamant that Christ represented the only way to achieve salvation and freedom from sin and eternal damnation. The crusades and missionary expeditions sought to convert the heathens, whether Muslim, Hindu, Buddhist or Jew.

The report strongly queried this exclusive approach and spoke about the spiritual value within many religions and the genuine godliness of those who followed them. This report was welcomed by many as a great moral advance on the old doctrines. But accepting that other religions have insight into the divine and that it may not be necessary to become a Christian to enjoy the heavenly life once again raised monumental questions about the heart of Christian faith. What does this attitude imply about the status of Jesus Christ? Is he still seen as the Son of God? How important was his death on the cross, traditionally understood as the price for man's salvation, if non-Christians were right to praise their own God? These questions were never resolved because the report – though the subject of an internal discussion – was never widely debated or given doctrinal authority.

Many of the emerging discussions centred on Jesus and how to interpret his life and death. Stories about the historical figure of Jesus have abounded in recent years. Since the "Godspell" and "Jesus Christ Superstar" musicals, fascination about the first century carpenter has grown enormously. The film and television world has recreated the historical Jesus with great reverence for his human values as exemplified in the Sermon on the Mount.

But it has not been the human characteristics of Jesus which have been most critical for the Christian religion throughout history. He has been worshipped as the Son of God who came to earth to save mankind from its sins, performing miraculous deeds which revealed his divine origin and rising from the grave to prove his power over death.

It is these facets of the historical Jesus which became the central subject of dispute and controversy. While nearly all stood firm in rejecting the atheism of the 'God is Dead' thinkers, it became more and more clear that going beyond the affirmation of belief in God and on to express faith in Jesus as his Son was more problematic.

Like all theological disputes, there have been rumblings for decades and even centuries – with great minds pondering the imponderable – but rarely, if ever, has the Church and the nation become so enmeshed in such debates as in recent years. For events conspired to bring about an unparalleled public awareness of the problems of faith in Jesus Christ at the very time that many in the Church were becoming acutely disturbed about the loss of faith in Christianity in this country.

The catalyst was a television series called "Jesus: The Evidence", due to be broadcast over Easter, which promised to offer a sober investigation into the historical evidence about Jesus and the origins of the New Testament accounts of his life.

Before the series hit the air there were protests from evangelical Christian groups that the series was a deliberate assassination of the founder of the faith, and included allegations that he was a homosexual or possibly had never existed. The programme-makers, London Weekend Television, denied these allegations but the series went out under a cloud of smoke with the Christian world determined to resist its 'evidence'.

The series did not mention homosexuality and while it interviewed a Professor George Wells who claimed that Jesus had never existed, it then proceeded to demolish his arguments. But the protests continued apace long after the series had been broadcast because "Jesus: The Evidence" made damaging accusations about the historical status of Christ. It accumulated a mass of historical and scientific data which conflicted with the accounts of Jesus's life as recorded in the gospels. Drawing upon a wealth of biblical scholarship the programmes pointed out that the gospels were written long after Jesus's death by writers who had no personal knowledge of him. They went on to claim that much of the information recorded about his life was literally manufactured. The programmes homed in on the supernatural aspects of Jesus's life, casting strong doubt on the source of passages which refer to the virgin birth, miracles and resurrection.

With the aid of modern textual analysis the series focused upon alleged contradictions and inaccuracies throughout the New Testament, questioning their overall reliability as historical documents. In looking at the idea that Jesus had been born of a virgin, for example, the series explained that the word "virgin" written in Greek in Matthew's gospel had been mistakenly translated from a Hebrew word meaning simply "young girl." They also drew upon the findings of 19th century archaeologists who discovered the remains of many holy men from the Middle East, all of whom it was claimed had been born of a virgin.

The accumulative conclusion of "Jesus: The Evidence", though never stated, was unmistakable: that the historical figure was simply a wise and holy man who had been elevated into a God by miraculous additions to his life-story.

Christians across Britain — from the Oxbridge academic cloisters to the Baptist halls — condemned the series, with some of the most liberal biblical scholars pointing to historical weaknesses. But a student of the backlash could not have failed to notice the great chasm between the theologians' criticisms and those of Christian organisations. The powerful Evangelical Alliance viewed the series as a satanic enterprise with no redeeming features, while others like Professor Nineham of Bristol University demurred from the series on a few minor issues. The unity within the Christian world against "Jesus: The Evidence" fell apart as soon as the material within the series was closely examined.

That examination was started by LWT's own religious affairs programme CREDO which set out to assess how much of the 'evidence' the Church did accept. Professor David Jenkins was considered the ideal interviewee, being a respected academic who was known to stand in the middle ground of the world of theology. He was also a professing Christian and shortly to become the Bishop of Durham.

It was immediately obvious that Dr Jenkins had a far more traditional faith than Don Cupitt and some of the other radicals on the edge of the Church. He spoke not just of belief in God but of Jesus as God's last and greatest work, something which "gave him a unique relationship to God", and the belief built up that this was not just God doing something through him but God doing it as him. "There's a sense in which we have to re-understand God. God is not transcendent and beyond everything and doesn't just work through other agents, but he has so much love and is so down to earth that you can actually believe that there was a real sense in which God is Jesus and Jesus is God."

Despite this affirmation it became clear as the interview developed that Dr Jenkins was offering scant comfort to those traditionalists and evangelicals who dismissed all the difficulties raised by "Jesus: The Evidence." In particular, Dr Jenkins shared the series' scepticism about the factual basis of the miraculous aspects of Jesus's life. "I'm pretty clear that the virgin birth was a story told after the event in order to express and symbolize a faith that this Jesus was a unique event from God."

There is little doubt that this alone would have enraged many people, but it was the language Dr Jenkins used to describe his position which created the basis for the headlines and subsequent controversy. He continued, "I wouldn't put it past God to arrange a virgin birth if he wanted to, but I very much doubt if he would."

He offered a comparable account of the resurrection of Jesus, dismissing the idea that it was an actual physical event, being more sympathetic to the idea that the disciples witnessed a series of apparitions. Compounding this, he argued on a radio phone-in that the empty tomb which had been seen as proof of Jesus's resurrection could imply many different things. "Maybe," he proferred, "the disciples came and pinched the body."

The ensuing protests and public rows over his enthronement at York Minster clearly revealed how many Christians held on to a traditional understanding of the Christian faith. But overall Christian opinion within the country is harder to gauge. There is substantially the question of truth. Is Jesus the Son of God? Was he born of a virgin? Did he perform miracles? Did he rise from the dead? The evidence, though powerful, is not overwhelming either way and – as the contributors to this book recognise – a judgment about the significance of Jesus ultimately comes down to a question of faith.

21

From the outset the debates over Jenkins did not actually centre on questions of truth but on the likely impact on the Church of bishops expressing doubts about the faith. The argument ran that people are looking for certainty in these troubled times and that a Church which is itself riddled with doubt could have no hope of bringing the people back to Christian faith.

The evidence here is sketchy and by no means clear. Dr Jenkins proudly recounts how he heard two ladies in a cake shop discussing the meaning of Jesus's resurrection, convinced that he has made people think about Christianity for the first time in a long while. His postbag also supports his argument. For while one might expect most letter-writers to have been motivated by anger, even at the height of the controversy the mail was running three–one in his favour, with many writing to thank him for trying to grapple with beliefs which they found hard to accept today.

His postbag, in fact, echoed that of John Robinson who, as Bishop of Woolwich in the early 'sixties, created a similar controversy, suggesting in "Honest to God" that many traditional ideas about God had to be abandoned.

Robert Towler analysed the letters which John Robinson received, and concluded that people had a variety of religious dispositions such that, while some required absolute certainty and needed to be confident of the Church's orthodoxy, others were deeply affected by rational scepticism and enormously encouraged when Church leaders expressed their own uncertainty.

This is precisely why there is such an array of Christian Churches in Britain and throughout the world – they appeal to fundamentally different religious characters within people. Whether the Church of England can continue to appeal to a broad range of believers without appearing hopelessly contradictory is debatable.

SEARCHING FOR CERTAINTY

JOHN TINSLEY

John Tinsley was Bishop of Bristol from 1976 to 1985, having previously been the Professor of Theology at Leeds University. He studied English and Theology at Durham University where he gained a lifelong passion for literature. He worked in various parishes in the North East before returning to university to teach at Hull.

During his years as a Bishop he became increasingly concerned about the moves towards conservatism in both politics and religion and spoke out for a liberal under-standing of the Christian faith. His published works include "Tragedy, Irony and Faith" – a work on the role of tragedy in religion and literature – and "The Imitation of God" – a study of the role of Christ in Christian mysticism.

Christianity Direct and Indirect

The upsurge of dogmatism

In times of rapid social and intellectual change like our own people inevitably look round for something stable, fixed, certain. One has only to think of the bewildering changes in the sciences, technology and medicine to understand people's nostalgic hankering for a past where things are believed to have been secure and reliable. This is especially the case in religion, the popular image of which is of something that by its nature never changes – or never ought to – and remains the same yesterday, today and tomorrow. If they turn to the Church, people expect it to provide psychological security.

There is therefore a natural momentum in our day towards fixed and final dogma in religion, politics and ethics and a tendency to retreat into a private world where the language used supports the traditional structures of belief and worship and hardly resonates at all with the experience of ordinary people. Fundamentalist literalism of a kind which seeks to use scripture as an infallible oracle, all on one level of meaning – the literal – has increasing numbers of adherents in Judaism, Christianity and Islam. Examples are some of the fanatical sects in present-day Israel, the "Bible-belt" form of Christianity in the USA – and some British fundamentalism comes near to it – and the Islamic conservative revolution in Iran led by Ayatollah Khomeini. In politics there has been a return to a dogmatism of a similar kind based on either some sentimental fantasy about the past, the apparently self-evident purity of "nineteenth-century virtues", or rigid adherence to one fixed dogma such as monetarism which keeps on producing absurd postures of infallibility. In the field of ethics too there has been a revolt against liberality in favour of hard-line dogmatism and an unwillingness to re-examine established positions in the light of new knowledge.

So in general we can say that the more confused and uncertain the scene the more strident and insular becomes the dogmatic voice and the more the idea abounds that there is access somewhere to absolute certainty. But, as the Catholic thinker Hans Küng has put it: "It's often the most banal truths that have absolute certainty. The significance of a truth is in inverse ratio to its certainty". There is a particular momentum in the religions towards conservatism and they have not, generally speaking, been good at taking the initiatives and risks to enlarge the bounds of freedom in a creative way or to extend the range of toleration. Such moves have usually come from secular non-religious pressures. We shall soon be coming up, in 1989, to the two-hundredth anniversary of the French Revolution with its slogan of "liberty, fraternity and equality". We still have a long way to go, not least in the field of religion, before we reach anything like the attainment of these ideals.

It is worth while pondering on this quest for certainty and absolute truth and the desire to insulate oneself from uncomfortable facts and data, especially those produced by scientific experiment and historical research. Compounding the psychological need for certainty there are very strong authoritarian elements in those religious traditions which are based on the belief that God has revealed himself in historical events: Judaism, Christianity and Islam. There seems to be in these religions a natural momentum to assume that if God has revealed himself in historical events or persons, such revelation must be unmistakable, unquestionable and unambiguous. Much is made of such revelation being authoritative, as if it could be divested of fallible subjective interpretations. But the content of what is alleged to be divine revelation receives its particular shape from passing through human minds and imaginations. It would not be difficult to cite phases in the histories of Judaism, Christianity and Islam in which they claim that they have absolute, fixed and final truth of a unique kind and that other religions are the realm of the infidel, the heretic and the downright demonic.

With such an absolute claim to unique truth there is said to be no room for doubt about any part of traditional doctrine.

To doubt, it is assumed, would be to betray or to be disloyal. Since psychologically we seem built for trust and security there is an inevitable tendency to put absolute trust in what may be relative. In some popular handbooks for the faithful – I am thinking of confirmation manuals of a generation or so ago – 'doubt' was classed as a sin to be confessed and one was led to believe that it always denoted a feeble faith. But if we have any glimmering of the mystery of the being of God we must continuously doubt our capacity to express adequately or finally belief about God. There is no absolute dividing line between a world of belief and a world of doubt. There is always a dialogue going on in each person between belief and doubt along the lines of the words of the father of the epileptic boy in St Mark: "Lord, I believe, help my unbelief". As "The Cloud of Unknowing", a superb English fourteenth-century mystical treatise puts it: "God may well be loved, but he may not be thought of". Even our best professions of faith have only provisional and temporary status. This goes for all creeds, decrees of Church Councils or papal pronouncements. Christian agnosticism of this kind, far from being a culpable aberration, is a deep-seated necessity if there is to be any humility, honesty and reverence in religion. Indeed faith needs the company of doubt and agnosticism. Left to itself faith is capable of its own characteristic excesses. It can believe too much and too indiscriminately, ending up in sheer credulity. Faith needs the continuous ministry of unbelief to purify it from the inevitable accumulation of second-hand and obsolete religious thoughts and habits, and to purge it of the inferior consolations and hopes of sentimentality.

There is always a difference between what professional theologians say the beliefs of a particular religion are, and what actually goes on at the popular level. Ordinary people draw their theology more from favourite hymns than books of theology. Furthermore there are always at least two main versions of any religion. In Christianity, for instance, there is the version which sees itself as a universal truth needing to be related continually to all aspects and developments of human thought and experience. There is also a version of Christianity which sees itself as principally and exclusively concerned with 'spiritual values', expressing itself in personal piety, 'simple trust', unquestioning acceptance. There is on the one hand, then, the Christianity which, since the rise of science and scientific thinking and the dramatic change in the picture of the universe that this has brought about, seeks as a matter of religious duty to explore what this implies for the understanding and expression of Christian belief. On the other hand, there is the Christianity which shuts itself away from all this, behaves as if scientific and historical research had never happened, and shouts more and more stridently the old slogans, irrespective of the social and political issues of the day. It is this latter version of Christianity which seems to be getting the upper hand. What we now have is a deepening divide between those who, like the Hebrew prophets, find God the great disturber of our complacencies and conventions, especially in religion, and those for whom God is always and ever the soother and supporter.

Behind all the present-day clamour for definite teaching and straight answers there is a fundamental theological issue at stake, nothing less than the question of the kind of God that is believed in and the way he makes himself known.

The two types of Christianity referred to each have a distinctive theology and concept of evangelism. Each has its own idea of the kind of revelation which has taken place. The first we can call 'revelation direct'. This assumes that the meaning of Christ was originally quite clear and capable of being stated in the simplest and most direct prose. Christian evangelism must therefore be correspondingly direct and explicit. All that prevents people accepting it is wilful ignorance or perverse obtuseness. We will be told that the problem is apathy. The assumption is that the only thing getting in the way of the spread of Christianity is moral, intellectual or spiritual lethargy. Or we will be told that the main problem is that Christian preachers are unable to express the gospel with sufficient clarity, if only they were able to put it across more effectively conversion would follow. Here again is the assumption that the original Jesus of Nazareth was easily understandable first time round and that subsequent proclamation of him is primarily a matter of simplified assertion. One is reminded of the comments of

29

politicians after defeat in a general or by-election, when failure will be put down to inability to get the message across clearly.

As far as this type of Christianity is concerned the eighteenth-century Enlightenment might never have happened. A favourite manoeuvre is to dub as out of date all critical questioning of a scientific or historical character such as one associates with the Enlightenment. The impression is given that all these questions have been answered, whereas they have either not been faced or have been side-tracked. In 'Christianity direct', for example, the bible is used as if critical literary and historical research on it had never happened and as if there are no serious questions raised by the indirect Christ of St Mark and the direct Christ of St John.

There is all the difference between those religious traditions that have experienced and faced the questions posed by the Enlightenment and those that have yet to do so. When these questions about the nature of authority, the implications of historical evidence and research, the role of scientific experimentation, and the rational element in religious belief have been faced things can never be the same again. A Christianity which has faced these questions must henceforth know, among other things, how to handle the probabilities and ambiguities of history. Historical study of the New Testament gospels, for example, makes it clear that the gospel of Christ cannot be condensed into a number of simple abstract propositions which one can then use deductively, but is a personal style exhibited by Jesus himself as a "sign of the times". It is also clear that the teaching and work of Jesus were closely related to the social and political realities of his day, and if Christianity is to echo the kind of gospel which he embodies this must appear in the content, tone and manner of speech about him. Consequently Christian evangelism is not best thought of as a clarion call or recall to the lapsed and indifferent but it must show pretty prominently a use of reason, imagination and dialogue which reveal convincingly that the questions and problems have been faced, and that it can embrace with evident understanding serious and informed unbelief.

30

The trouble with 'Christianity direct' and the fundamentalist literalist interpretation of the bible on which it mostly rests, is that it flies in the face of the manner of God's revelation of himself that the biblical writers are at pains to emphasize. In a way which is in fact alien to the bible in both Old and New Testaments people have assumed that if God reveals himself as he is said to do in the history of Israel and the history of Christ, it must necessarily, since it is the revelation of God, have been unmistakable, indisputable, authoritarian and universally apparent. God just must be the one who dictates infallibly, never leaving room for any dubiety. One of the effects of the casual use of 'Almighty God' may be to suggest this image of a God who is by nature and in revelation imperious.

Consequently we have produced what may be called the heresy of the paraphrase, paraphrase meaning here the attempt to simplify and indeed replace a subtle and many-sided original, for which the paraphrase can be a substitute. Such a search for paraphrase lies behind the assumption that the bible as a whole or Christianity can be paraphrased simply into a gist, essence or message. We hear the phrase 'The bible says' or are given the 'essence of Christianity'. If faith and imagination have gone into the original, as they most certainly have in metaphor and parable in both Old and New Testaments, it is a serious tampering with the original to separate them by substituting some prose paraphrase.

God's indirect revelation

The bible is a radical and revolutionary reversal of our normal preconceptions about God and how he acts in history and in human life. There is a firm biblical base for the belief that the original revelatory acts of God in Israel and in Christ are best described as personal since they always have the innuendoes, the equivocal and indirect manner of the sort of personal dealings which love and respect freedom and integrity. The strongest currents in both Testaments run in this direction and lead one to the conclusion that the kind of

31

revelation witnessed to in the bible is indirect rather than direct. In fact, in the Old Testament indirect revelation is already on an altogether higher plane of reality and significance than direct. The history of Israel is presented in the Old Testament as that of a people finding it necessary to move from early crude ideas of direct theophanies to the awareness of a God who hides himself and whose glory it is to conceal things. The Old Testament is hesitant, to say the least, about direct revelation, direct knowledge and direct sight of God. "No one shall see God and live" is a constant refrain. Even an exceptional person like Moses is granted in the end what the Hebrew text quaintly calls sight of the "backside" of God. The characteristic Hebrew vision of God's manner in revelation is well illustrated in the famous dialogue between Moses and God on the question of how God is to be identified with certainty in life. Moses asks who he shall say has sent him when he is asked by the people to authenticate the divine call to leave Egypt. How can he give the people a clear definite reply? Back comes the answer of God, not well translated in our older English versions as "I am that I am". A more accurate translation of the Hebrew would be: "I will be what I will be". I will be there in the future what I have been there in the past. Never mind: get on with life. I will show myself in my own time and way. I will be known in the journeying. There is no direct, indisputable, unambiguous sign of the presence of God. There are always other, ordinary and less demanding, "explanations" for what some take as the "signs of God" – it could be only coincidence. In a similar way of indirection Elijah has to be weaned away from the notion that God is directly in "the wind, or the earthquake or the fire". No, he is ambiguously and elusively in "the still small voice".

God's way of revelation in the Old Testament is best perceived in the form of personal dialogue. Not surprisingly, therefore, much of the Old Testament literature is in the form of dialogue between God and human beings, sometimes very strenuous as for example where God and Job argue it out as to why, in terms of God's own justice, there is so much cruelty and suffering. The "Word of God" in the Old Testament which is seen as coming to human beings is a truly

32

personal, listening speech which talks through situations, events and experiences in such a way that we become aware of what Bishop Ian Ramsey called "disclosure situations" where "the penny drops" and we see clearly, or see again with a new clarity or depth the meaning of something with which we have been long familiar.

God's revelation in Jesus of Nazareth has the same indirect character in the New Testament. The characteristic manner of Jesus as presented in the earlier tradition about him, especially in St Mark's gospel, would lead one to describe him as 'a prophet of indirect communication'. Jesus saw in what was happening in his own day what he called "signs of the times", signs of the coming of the "Kingdom of God", but how and where the "Kingdom of God" was coming he cannot state explicitly but can only indicate in parabolic word and parabolic action. The "Kingdom of God", he says, does not come "with observation" of the kind that enables one to say with certainty "Here it is" or "There it is". Nevertheless the Kingdom of God "is amongst you" and Jesus indicates pointedly that the story of his times is on one level a history of the day and on another level, for those with the imaginative insight to see, the coming of the "Kingdom of God". He sees these signs himself and expects his contemporaries to see them too. Hence his refrain about having "eyes to see and ears to hear".

God's manner in Christ may therefore be described as authoritative but not authoritarian. It is indirect, elusive, enigmatic, parabolic. This is the basis of 'Christianity indirect' which is absolute in its commitment to truth without being totalitarian in attitude or pronouncement. Therefore any style of Christian evangelism which browbeats rather than elicits, which is self-asserting and not self-effacing, which has vulgarity and ostentation instead of awe and simplicity, which seeks popularity and "success" at all costs and not the stark grandeur of truth, is a violation of the very gospel to which it is supposed to be witnessing and is guilty of turning a 'sign' into what Jesus would have called a 'stumbling-block'.

Christianity may have begun with this indirect style but there is early evidence that the Church became restless with it as it sought to structure itself on a parable. As one writer has put it: "You cannot found a state religion or a practical homiletic upon a collection of riddles". The human spirit is impatient with the ambiguity of parable.

St Mark's gospel soon proved to be impossibly indirect and ambiguous for the early Church. A detailed study of the gospels of Matthew and Luke clearly shows them again and again making explicitly direct what was ambiguous in original Mark. The whole process of the transmission of the material about Jesus from St Mark to St John is a case of moving the story of Jesus from its original ambiguity to something more evident and obvious.

Certainly a first reading of St John would give the impression that this process of de-mystification is complete. Everything now seems to be authoritarian, direct, un-equivocal, non-parabolic. The Christian tradition has had to pay a very heavy price for taking the teaching of Jesus as given in St John only on one level of meaning – the literal one – and building on it dogmas about the person of Christ. St John's was the most influential of the gospels on the formation of Christian doctrine, and even today questions about the humanity of Jesus or the meaning of his 'divinity' are often assumed to be settled by quoting sayings from St John's gospel like "I and the Father are one". But St John's gospel was not written to be read in this way. The author makes it quite clear that he is going over the story of Jesus again in the perspective of the resurrection, which gives the gospel, to Christian believers who are thus put in the know, a constant irony as the evangelist pointedly contrasts what appears to be going on at the surface level of observable fact and the deeper significance available to those not taken in by appearances but who see beyond the letter. "The letter kills, the Spirit gives life". The author has written a life of Christ to make it clear that "Christ" now means, for the Christian believer, not only the Jesus of Nazareth of past history, but the Christ now of present eucharistic experience, and also the Christ who is to come. And all three at once, because in a masterly way he has blended together the three primary tenses of past, present and future in the simultaneous now of worship. The irony of a wooden literalistic use of St John's gospel is that this book is an evident diatribe against such fundamentalist, unimaginative and indeed unliterary interpretation of the teaching of Jesus. One could take as an example the sequence in chapters 2–4 on detecting signs of the presence of God. Here "the Jews", in their role in this gospel as fundamentalists, ask for a sign when one has just been given, and solemnly argue the literal absurdity of Christ's claim to build a temple: "it has taken 46 years to build this temple, will you raise it up in 3 days?" For Christian readers of the gospel who are in the know, the words of Jesus about the temple refer not to the obvious appearances but to hidden realities. "He spoke of the temple of his body", says the evangelist, with the characteristic reminder that it is the perspective of the resurrection which enables the reader to see the ironic character of the actions and words of Jesus during his actual lifetime. "When, therefore, he was raised from the dead", continues the evangelist, "his disciples remembered that he had said this and they believed" as you too, readers, will believe, he infers, who have been given the clue to see the irony of things. This is followed by the dialogue with Nicodemus, another fundamentalist, who professes to see the signs that are being given, but proceeds at once to literalise what Jesus says about being "born again". This leads into the dialogue with the Samaritan woman at Jacob's well. Once again the reader is nudged by the evangelist to see the irony of the situation. Jesus's request for water is subjected by the woman to a most literal analysis by which the evangelist underlines the irony of Jesus who is himself the source of living water asking for a drink, and the woman who gives him water is the one who herself most needs the living water which only he can give. St John's gospel turns out to be a most subtle presentation of the indirectness of Christ.

Sign and miracle

The treatment of miracle in the gospels corroborates this interpretation of the method of God in Christ as being indirect. Indeed the gospels suggest that Jesus had his own distinctive attitude to 'miracles' in the modern sense of prodigious violations of known laws of nature. Only one of the words translated 'miracle' in the gospels means an astonishing, extraordinary reversal of the ordinary. The other words used refer to an event which at one and the same time can be taken by some as a perfectly ordinary incident and by others as pointing in a transcendental direction. Such events raise questions of moral commitment as part of their interpretation. Jesus seems to have been suspicious of the prodigy type of 'miracle' and discouraged the expectation of it, being himself much more concerned with insight and receptivity in the way we respond to the ordinary and familiar: "having eyes do you not yet see, and having ears do you not yet hear?".

Whatever the happenings were that Jesus identified as tokens of God's activity in his time, they were not 'miracles' in the modern sense. They were not, to use a phrase from the gospels, "signs from heaven". In fact to seek for such 'miracles' was for Jesus the mark of "an evil and adulterous generation". No such sign, says Jesus, will be given to his generation. It is also significant that the 'miraculous' is never an element in that form of his teaching where it might have been expected, namely his parabolic stories. In fact the end of his parable of the rich man and Lazarus is all of a piece with his general attitude of discouraging the idea that the truth of religious belief could be established by some 'miracle' like a raising from the dead: "if they do not hear Moses and the prohets neither will they be convinced if one should rise from the dead".

Christ's vision of God could only be indicated in parabolic speech and action. The temptation narratives show a Christ who puts aside the idea of miraculous certainty as Satanic. 'Miracles' in the sense of open indisputable wonders would have been alien to the mind, purpose and beliefs of Jesus. In the light of this we need to redefine the meaning of 'miracle'. In the words of a Swiss scholar: "A divine action of quite ordinary appearance, visible only to the believer is a miracle. On the contrary, a phenomenon which is extraordinary, amazing, inexplicable but unrelated to faith is not one".

The present ferment in the Church about the state of doctrine is not a matter of updating ancient orthodoxy to fit in with modern thought. It is about a fresh understanding of the nature of the revelation of God in Christ. The structural necessities of the Church have an inbuilt tendency to get in the way of free response to Christ as the parable of God. The ambiguities of the 'sign' get replaced by the so-called certainties of miraculous 'proofs'. 'Christianity direct' overwhelms 'Christianity indirect'. An ambiguous Christ is replaced by an authoritarian Christ. The 'stumbling-block' is removed from the 'sign' and only an alleged unassailable and invulnerable certainty remains.

We are living again in the situation classically defined in Dostoevsky's famous legend of the Grand Inquisitor in his "The Brothers Karamazov". In the story Christ returns to sixteenth-century Seville and is almost immediately imprisoned, brought to trial and charged with the great crime of having given human beings freedom. "Instead of taking possession of men's freedom," says the Grand Inquisitor, "you multiplied it and burdened the spiritual kingdom of man with its sufferings for ever. You wanted man's free love so that he should follow you freely . . . You did not want to enslave man by miracle because you hungered for a faith based on free will and not on miracles". You ask too much of human beings, continues the Grand Inquisitor; they really want to be told what to do and have their believing done for them. We therefore believe it to be our urgent mission "to relieve human beings of their great anxiety and of their present terrible torments of coming to a free decision themselves".

This story of the Grand Inquisitor is more than a brilliant feat of the imagination. It is a permanent reminder of the difficulties Christianity has experienced and is still experiencing of relating genuine freedom of enquiry to the commitment of faith. Dostoevsky's story is an extended commentary on the saying of Christ in St John's gospel: "You seek me, not because you saw signs, but because you ate your fill of the loaves". Humanity will have its miracles in spite of the strictures of Christ himself.

COLIN BUCHANON

Colin Buchanon has been Bishop of Aston since 1985. For 21 years he taught at a theological college, training people for the Anglican ministry. He is one of a new generation of evangelical leaders who projects the traditional gospel message with an openness and humour which appeals to many across the Church.

He is sympathetic to the Charismatic Movement and has written extensively on Christian worship through his own publishing company, Grove Booklets.

The Message of Salvation

I am an old-fashioned Christian believer. No doubt I am influenced by being British, affected by pricks and nudges on my life in my teens and early twenties in ways which would not have been readily available to a Chinese peasant or a Sikh trader. But I am not one who has believed the Christian faith entire throughout my life, and I have, in a gentle way, had an adult conversion. At that point in my life I was also confirmed in the Church of England, which involved a conscious positive step away from my nominally Free Church background. I may be the child of my context and circumstances (who knows?), but I have given some thought and study to the question of Jesus Christ, and some consequent bending of the will and the mind to his authority over me. Clearly I start from a committed position – I only ask that readers note it was no light commitment, no unthinking surrender of my autonomy.

Truth

Anyone thinking Christianity through from scratch, or from doubt, is bound to ask 'what actually happened?' There is a current practice of Christianity which can be observed, but very slight enquiry soon reveals that the whole position is bound up with the person of Jesus Christ, about whom the New Testament scriptures give virtually all the objective evidence that there is. Christianity, it quickly appears, is bound up with the view taken of this Jesus – and those who take the risk of enquiring too closely are liable to find that what began as them seeking the truth, subtly, and perhaps undetectably, has become Truth seeking them. This risk should not deter honest seekers from seeking. But it is a risk.

Truth then is bound up with the history of places far off and times long ago. To many palates this has no appeal. History cannot figure in the interests of those who know only the present – unless of course desperate hunger ever causes them to disregard the test of what is appetizing, and instead go for what is nutritious. Whether they do or not, Christianity's claims are bound up with certain historical assertions, and they are open to the enquiry even of persons who acknowledge no vast need, but genuinely want to find out 'what happened?'.

If we then home in on the life and person of Jesus Christ, we inevitably find ourselves also driven to the Old Testament scriptures. There is a background and a context to the life of Jesus. The background is as broad as the fact of creation (which can be asserted by faith prior to the enquiry into 'how' it happened), and as specific as the names and roles of the prophets of the Northern Kingdom in the eighth century. It weaves in the universal sinfulness of mankind. It begins the promise of the Messiah. It traces out the steps by which God of old dealt with his people. It shows the possibilities and the limitations of this period of preparation.

Simply to accept the Old Testament would be to become a Jew. This is exactly how the first disciples of Jesus were; they were Jews, yes, but their Jewishness was being transformed by their knowing Jesus. The New Testament is added to the Old, and different (but clearly justifiable) perspectives on the Old arise. God had spoken in creation, and in the patriarchs, the Exodus from Egypt, and the establishing of his people in the land; he had spoken by the law and the prophets, but now it was clear that what he was saying pointed forward to Jesus the Messiah, and thus advertised that what he had so far said was not his final or complete word to the human race. "God . . . has in these last days spoken to us by his Son" says the writer to the Hebrews. Little wonder that Jesus is the 'Word', the 'Logos'. God was in Jesus expressing himself fully on earth, and by that expression was both pointing up the limitations of earlier expressions, and also indicating what on the truest analysis they actually expressed.

Who then was this Jesus? If we go looking at 'what actually happened?', we are driven back to the person of Jesus. And the person of Jesus is available to us supremely through the revelation in the pages of the New Testament. And there are some scholarly problems here. The four gospels date from 60–100 A.D. Not all the authors necessarily walked in the steps of Jesus on earth. All of them wrote long after the crucifixion (which may have taken place around 30 A.D.). All of them are in some way influenced by the need to 'shape' their presentations for didactic purposes. Some of them are very dependent upon earlier drafts by others (though there is much discussion about how these dependences can be established). It is open to anyone to argue that the slightly stylized (but oh-so-fresh) accounts have come adrift from the 'Jesus of history', and, influenced by current Church life, have written back into history that which represents the unrooted but strong faith of their own time. In Matthew and John we can go further, and detect a doctrinaire necessity that the accounts must take on a certain form in order that the particular scriptures may be fulfilled – possibly without the chief protagonists realizing that they are working out of such a necessity – the characters do not need to know, for the evangelist knows and it is the clue to his insight. He takes us behind the scenes, to show us the heavenly director of the drama at work – but in so doing he leaves questions about the reality of that which we actually see going on.

Without arguing the case at every point, I assert that I am totally unconvinced by such scholarly approaches. Selection there has been, yes. Borrowing from other sources there has been, yes. Stylizing for liturgical, homiletical and catechetical purposes there has been, yes. But at the centre of it all, there still walks the figure of Jesus Christ as we have always known him. The scriptural accounts do have what J.B. Phillips called the "ring of truth" – but that might be dismissed as subjective. More to the present point, the documents stand up as historical documents. Indeed when I was an undergraduate reading Roman history, I found that my far-from-Christian tutor wanted to lay much more stress on the historicity of the Acts of the Apostles than the teachers of theology were generally ready to do. The documents themselves demand a verdict. To give them even provisional credence is to plunge oneself into dealings with this Jesus Christ. And the only Jesus Christ we can know is the one who lives in, and through, the gospel accounts of him. We go back to those accounts to discover him. And if we go back to them we encounter him.

Jesus Christ

It has been said that, based on the most scrupulous way of distinguishing one day from another, we only know of about twenty different days in the life of Jesus Christ. The weight of the gospel narratives lies towards the end – the passover at Jerusalem at which Jesus died occupies about one-third of each of the four Gospels, and gives us about six of the twenty days noted. Clearly the patterning is to direct us to the end.

That said, we can understand why the accounts of the beginning vary. There were thirty 'hidden years'. Save for the one mention of Jesus at the age of twelve, there is complete silence about those years. In dramatic terms he burst on the scene as an itinerant preacher at the age of thirty, with little previous publicity. The gospels are selective for all sorts of reasons – and dramatic presentation is one of those reasons. All four agree that the drama flows with both continuity and inevitability from the baptism of John and the revealing of Jesus to the final passover week and the death on the cross. (The cross is not the end, of course, but that is not the point of the current discussion). How should 'birth-narratives' fit into this continuity and inevitability? To Mark they would be a distraction; he begins with the ministry of John the Baptist. To John the birth is seen from a rather more cosmic standpoint – but it is there, knit to the rest of the story by the shift of the observer's viewpoint as he moves gently to "we beheld his glory". To Matthew and Luke the narratives are needed, though there remains a discontinuity. In Matthew the element of continuity comes from the overall sense that the scriptures (that is, the Old Testament scriptures) 'must' be fulfilled. In Luke that element is provided by the dramatic oscillation between the events surrounding John the Baptist, and those surrounding Jesus. There are two 'annunciations'; first that to Zechariah, then that to Mary. Then there are two birth stories; first that of John, then that of Jesus. And this pattern leads into the start of the continuous story, where there is first the ministry of the forerunner, then that of Jesus. In each case, the Jesus event is weightier, more significant, and more far-reaching, than the John one. But in each case John comes first. None of the four gospel-writers was attempting a chronicled camera-recorded look at each day in Jesus's life, and each presents selected material for his own purposes. Paul too, when he reflects on Jesus, writes like a man who knew the balance of presentation in the Gospels. That no more means he was ignorant of the manner of Jesus's birth than his failure to mention Pilate by name means he was ignorant of the manner of Jesus's death.

Thus the question of the manner of Jesus's birth must be handled as one of subsidiary importance for the purposes of the gospel-writers. If, however, we persist with our question of 'what actually happened?' (a question, it seems to me, that they would have understood, for all that they wanted to interpret the event and use it homiletically), then the answer is there to hand. Matthew and Luke agree that Jesus was conceived by a virgin mother, without initially the knowledge or consent of Joseph to whom she was betrothed, and that both Joseph and Mary learned miraculously that her child would be the Son of God, the 'Saviour' (which is what 'Jesus' means). We get little hint as to why the Son of God should come on earth in this way, and thus we are left to wrestle with the significance and importance of the event in a speculative way. But one useful line of speculation lies in the area of Jesus's pre-existence: the normal processes of conception lead to the birth of a new being, whereas this unique process was being used by God for the 'in-carn-ation' of one who already existed. This undergirds all questions about the person of Jesus Christ, and faithfully reflects the theological insistence of the Letter to the Hebrews that he was "brought into the world" and was "made like us" – the pre-existence and the true identification with the human race are both deeply emphasized in the Letter to the Hebrews, and each is an integral part of the 'message of salvation'. It is the God-man who reaches from God to man, and whose grasp does not slip at either end of his reach.

The greater emphasis of the New Testament is upon the person of Jesus, grown to thirty years of age and walking through Galilee and up to Jerusalem, conscripting followers, teaching startling truths in a down-to-earth manner – and causing many to go into opposition to him. Here is the focus of much of the four Gospels – teaching, encounters, parables, miracles: these are features of the account. And his teaching is in many ways a 'message of salvation'. When Zacchaeus turns from his greed to acknowledge Jesus as his Lord, then "salvation is come to this house". And when others are physically healed and 'made whole', it is the same 'salvation' word which is used of being healed. And in the parable of the lost sheep, "The Son of Man has come to seek and to save that which was lost". There is a 'lost-ness' about the human race, and Jesus, the 'Son of Man', has come to 'find' or to 'save' the lost – to bring them home to his Father. God became man to bring man to God, and it is by the person of God the Son that we are reconciled to our creator and know him as Father.

Clearly the thrust of the Gospels is towards that last passover week in Jerusalem. Jesus has made it clear that he goes to Jerusalem to die, and there he duly goes. The disciples go with him. On the Thursday night he holds his 'Last Supper' with the disciples, he is betrayed, arrested, and after a manner tried. His death follows as predicted. But amid all the weight upon the trial, and even the words of Jesus at Calvary, there is a great reticence about the physical suffering – "there they crucified him" is the limit of the description. Rather, the reader is left to puzzle as to why he endured this death. At this point the question 'what actually happened?' can be answered with considerable accuracy, but little usefulness. We need to know why.

It will be no news to any reader of this that the Christian belief is that Jesus's death was instrumental in bringing us back to God. That belief is based upon an all-pervading teaching of the New Testament, much of it from the earliest records of all – Paul's letters. Book after book adds weight to the united story – "In due time Christ died for the ungodly", "Christ died for sins once for all, the righteous for the unrighteous, to bring you to God". Under the cloak of the darkness at mid-day, to which the gospel-writers refer, in some mysterious and imagination-defying way, the sins of the world were taken into the body, indeed into the person, of Jesus. And 'what actually happened?' must be answered at the level of this astonishing redemption or ransoming, as well as at the physical level of the knocking in of the nails.

The scriptures are very clear that if this had been the end, then the story would hardly have been worth telling to its end. An itinerant prophet, who duly caught it in the neck, might be remembered for some quotable maxims like "take no thought for tomorrow", but his death would be of no special noteworthiness. Indeed, his earlier predictions that on the third day he would rise again would then stand to discredit him. His death becomes significant only because he rose again, and the significance of his death is then established as 'saving', and not just as setting a heroic example of non-resistance to evil.

For on the third day the tomb was empty. The disciples were convinced he had risen simply by the sight of that empty tomb, even before they met him alive. When Peter preached in the open-air on the day of Pentecost, he contrasted the respect held for King David of old, whose tomb was still to be seen in Jerusalem, and the total claims upon their lives of this Jesus, who had been raised from the dead, and for whom, fifty days after the passover, no tomb can be shown. There had been a place where his body had been laid – that is true. But something had meant that, in effect, there was now no tomb. He had been raised from the dead. And, once again, 'what actually happened' had several layers of exposition to it. Yes, one came back from the dead – and a Jewish writer has recently acknowledged this to be true, even whilst uncertainties have been found among Christians. But Peter's assertion was that "God raised him from the dead". Paul's word is that, by the resurrection from the dead, Jesus was declared to be the Son of God with power. And when John the Divine sees a vision of Christ in glory, saying to him "I was dead and behold I am alive for evermore", this is at the heart of Christianity. The Jesus Christ to whom Christians respond is not the dead (though appealing) person of the past, but the living Lord of the present. He is the same Jesus Christ who is presented to us in the gospels; he teaches the same truths, displays the same love, and exercises the same power to draw men and women after him – but he does so from his living reigning position "at the right hand of the Father". This Jesus we proclaim, and give our lives up to proclaiming.

Faith

What then do we do, responding to Jesus Christ, for our salvation? The message of Christ must tell us exactly what to do. Otherwise there might be information, there might be data for speculation, but there would be no message.

And the message has already been creeping through in all the discussion above about Jesus himself. It is impossible to present him without presenting his purpose in coming to earth. It is impossible to present his purpose without hinting at how it not only objectively provides salvation for us, but also personally is received by us. There are great objective facts of God's mighty acts in creation and in history; but there is also a further mighty act when God takes over the life of this man and that woman. There is a contemporary ongoing work being wrought by God to bring people into the experience of salvation, and to ensure that his Church – that is, his people – will never perish from the earth. If this work is to go forward, how does the salvation come to each generation, indeed to each person?

From Genesis onwards, the scriptures teach that God, by his power and his love, gives his gifts to human beings not as a reward for what they have done, but as a free gift. All that is needed on the human side is faith. "By grace you are saved through faith" is a very succinct Pauline statement of God's way of salvation. It is explicit in the earlier quotation above, "In due time Christ died for the ungodly". Had it read that 'Christ died for the godly' (or for the righteous, or for the meritorious, or even for the rich or the aristocrats) then the forgiveness of Jesus's death would have been given as a reward for the virtues displayed by these selected recipients. But if he died for the "ungodly", then it is clear that nothing in us deserved his favour.

So we are confined to sheer faith as the means of receiving God's free gift. This faith is simply the willingness to open an empty hand and see God pour his gifts into it. It is not itself a meritorious work. It is certainly not a cause of God's goodness. It is not even a 'triggering' of it. It is the mere receiving of the person of Jesus, and all he brings, into one's life. We do not move God to be good to us – we submit to the hammer-blows of love upon the doors of our life, and we find ourselves belonging to him.

It has been possible at times to think of faith as mere mental assent to a proposition. But 'saving' faith is not just believing that once in the past Christ died for me. It is not even believing that there is one God and that he revealed himself in Jesus Christ. It is not 'believing that' in any shape or form. It is 'believing in' or 'believing on' the living Christ. Faith is an entrusting of oneself to this Lordship – and Saviourhood – of Jesus: it is trusting Jesus Christ for salvation.

Points of origin

If this is the message of salvation, to whom is it applicable? Or to what sort of persons does it come? The traditional answer to this is that the good news (the gospel) is for sinners. Only those who know they are sinful will seek God's way of escape. But it is not quite as simple as that. The starting points vary enormously and we have to begin where people are: in moral dilemmas; or the purposelessness of life; or the fear of death; or the magnetism of Jesus Christ.

However, it is a Christian conviction that in principle all kinds of people in all kinds of need are met at their point of need by the gospel. In other words, if it is the purposelessness of life which, under the Holy Spirit, nudges a person towards Christ, then conversion will bring the discovery both of a purpose for life and also of the sense of sin, which is integral to the gospel but was not necessarily the point of origin of the conversion. Equally, receiving the Christian gospel may be accompanied by 'signs and wonders' – particularly healings – in line with the manifestations in the New Testament. Indeed, there are assemblies which demonstrate just this kind of miracle being worked by God. Great theological questions are raised by this, and we remain mortal men and women, with a brief uncertain licence to live on this earth. It is possible for dying men and women – and we are all dying men and women – to turn to Christ, and put their main hopes in the world to come. To revert to the theme with which this paragraph began: if a person desires physical healing, and comes to Christ with that hope, and is not physically healed, he or she may still be discovering that Jesus Christ which meets the deepest actual needs.

Points of arrival

I have yet to mention a whole dimension to the message of salvation which is central to the bible's history. It is hard to convey nowadays, as the break-up of Christendom in the West has left such a scattered and splintered pattern of congregational life, but it is vital.

The basic assertion is that the gospel creates a community. The first disciples exemplified this, the infant Church continued the pattern, the theological arguments of Paul reinforce it, and the ideal is thus set for us to hold before us. Put in the most simple terms, the new converts of the apostolic age were converted 'into the community'. It was not that they were converted one week, then shopped around for a good church to join the next. As like as not, they were originally touched by the gospel through the loving witness of the Christian community, and knew from this that a community was integral to the gospel – that God was calling a 'new people' for himself. They were thus baptized not only in submission to the gospel, but also in order to be transplanted into the community. Being converted and joining the community were the same thing! But nowadays we have lost sight of this – conversion tends to be an individualistic step of responding to the claims and call of Christ, which leads to the convert living an individualistic Christian life, until such time as he or she chooses to join this or that congregation or assembly. The whole range of choice of denomination seems alien to the given unity of the assemblies of the New Testament. The message of salvation establishes saved communities, and latter-day Western Christianity seems to have forgotten this.

Points of hope

The full revelation of the scriptures gives us a future hope. Christ will come again – or, if our own deaths anticipate that, we shall die "in the Lord" and depart to "be with Christ, which is far better". Paul wrote that if our hope in Christ only extended to this life, then we are of all people most to be pitied. We have a vision of heavenly glory – undeserved, but part of God's saving of us. This means that ageing and dying are received as part of God's good design for us. We wait, like watchmen staring into the darkness, peering for first signs of dawn.

The Christian people believe that they thus live in a tension between this world and the world to come. The world to come has already invaded this world in the person of Christ. His resurrection and ascension have given us pledges of our resurrection to eternal life. We love him, and our hearts are set on that which is 'not yet'.

Nevertheless, we are bound by a present duty – a duty that we should ourselves model the world to come, and ourselves be those who represent the breaking into this present world of the world to come. So we live in this world, as those who are not of it. And our so living is not just a preservation from contamination but a sign of the Kingdom of God to those around. And our gospel message therefore includes not only the urging to cleave to Christ, nor only the insistence that converts belong by their conversion to the people of God in a corporate way. We also proclaim a life of discipleship, a costly life, a life lit by the gift of the Holy Spirit, a life which is touched by the heavenly glory, and seeks to transform this world into the likeness of Christ's Kingdom. Discipleship involves taking up one's cross, denying oneself, and following steadfastly in the footsteps of the Master. That is full salvation indeed.

IAN WILSON

Ian Wilson is a writer who is most widely known for his worldwide investigation into the origin and authenticity of a burial cloth allegedly worn by Jesus, known as the Turin Shroud. His book of the same name has sold several million copies. He moved from agnosticism to a liberal Roman Catholic faith in 1970 and has since specialised in examining the status of religious phenomena.

In 1984 he wrote a critical account of the historical basis of the New Testament gospels, entitled "Jesus: The Evidence" which accompanied London Weekend Television's controversial series of the same name. Other books include "Mind out of Time?" and "The Exodus Enigma."

The Evidence for Jesus

Most committed Christians quite naturally think of 'Christ' as an ever-present, other-worldly entity, a living force in everyday lives. That is how vicars and priests refer to him in their sermons. And although the historical reality of Christ as Jesus of Nazareth is properly central to Christian thinking, it is often quite difficult for anyone, Christian or non-Christian, readily to envisage him as a genuinely flesh and blood human being of two thousand years ago. We have become all too familiar with the whiter– than– white Sunday school picture book image. And modern film-makers have provided surprisingly little service, even the Jesus of Zeffirelli's "Jesus of Nazareth" having a cardboard cut-out, not quite human quality that somehow fails to convince.

This raises the serious question, was there ever a historical Jesus of Nazareth? While it might seem obvious that there was, in fact the answer is by no means as straightforward as it might at first appear. There have of course been the more bizarre arguments for Jesus' non-existence, among these John Allegro's "The Sacred Mushroom and the Cross", claiming that the earliest so-called Christianity was all a cover for a secret cult of the sacred mushroom. Among many Communists Jesus is explained away as mythical leader of what had originally been an early proletarian communist movement.

But there have also been more serious scholarly attempts to disprove Jesus's historicity. The historian Lord Dacre, formerly Oxford's Regius Professor of Modern History, and well known for his involvement in the Hitler Diaries fiasco, has stated with ostensible authority in a Spectator review that there is no evidence for Jesus's existence before the fourth century AD. And the most formidable attack in recent years has come in the form of no less than three books by Birkbeck College Professor of German G.A. Wells: "The Jesus of the Early Christians", "Did Jesus Exist?" and most recently "The Historical Evidence for Jesus".

As pointed out by Professor Wells, most New Testament scholars are agreed that the gospels were written after the epistles of Paul. This is indeed the general consensus. As also noted by Wells, in these Pauline writings 'Christ' seems already a rather other-worldly figure, with scant suggestion that he was a real-life historical figure. There is no reference to the circumstances of Jesus's birth, no mention of his crucifixion in the time of Pontius Pilate. Paul does not even seem to show any apparent awareness of Jesus's unusual parables and acts of healing. This too is an accurate observation. For Wells, therefore, the trump card to Jesus's non-historicity has seemed to lie in the writings of the prolific first century Jewish historian Josephus. Since these contain no mention of Jesus except for what most recognize as a transparently latter-day interpolation by a mediaeval Christian scribe, the obvious logical deduction is that there never was any historical Jesus. He was simply invented by the gospel writers to give apparent flesh to the otherwise mythical figure created by Paul. In other words the whole foundation of Christianity is nothing more than a sham.

Adding some force to Wells's arguments is the undeniable fact that the gospels are disconcertingly vague and even contradictory concerning the exact dates of Jesus's birth and death. For instance, only two gospels contain accounts of the circumstances of Jesus's birth, Matthew's and Luke's. According to Matthew, Jesus was born "at Bethlehem in Judaea during the reign of king Herod", this Herod being Herod the Great, who is known to have ruled Judaea, Idumaea and Samaria between 37 and 4 BC. If Matthew is to be believed, Jesus must therefore have been born sometime during or before 4 BC. But according to Luke, Jesus's birth was at the time of a census when "Quirinius was governor of Syria". Since this census of Quirinius is a relatively well-attested historical event, specially noted by the Jewish historian Josephus to have taken place in the first year that Judaea came under direct Roman rule, which we now know as AD 6, the inference is unavoidable that either Matthew's or Luke's gospel, or possibly both, must be wrong. As for the idea that Jesus was born in 1 AD, i.e. the first year of the Christian calendar we have inherited through the centuries,

Rem: ✗ not unavoidable: if one considers the evidence from the point of view of a believer".

this derives from a simple miscalculation made by a Byzantine monk called Dionysius Exiguus, who was responsible for planning the Christian calendar back in the sixth century AD.

If it might be hoped that at least the date of Jesus's death has been better established, again the available information is at best confused. There is general agreement among the gospel writers that Jesus was crucified in the time of the Roman governor Pontius Pilate, whose term of administration is known to have been between 27 and 36 AD. A further clue to the year should be available from the gospel information that Jesus was crucified on the day before a Sabbath, i.e. on a Friday, and that Jesus's Last Supper (which would have to have been held on the Thursday evening), was a Passover meal, which Jews celebrate each year on the 14th Nisan of their calendar. Theoretically therefore, if we could tell in which year or years between 27 and 36 AD the 14th Nisan fell on a Thursday, we should be able to determine the year in which Jesus was crucified. But at this point whoever wrote the gospel of John confuses the issue. According to John it was the day of the crucifixion itself which was "Passover Preparation Day", i.e. the 14th Nisan. So if John is right, we should be looking for a year in which the 14th Nisan fell not on a Thursday but on a Friday.

An independent means of calculation seems to be offered by the information of Luke that John the Baptist's baptism of Jesus was "in the fifteenth year of Tiberius Caesar's reign", i.e. 29 AD, and since the synoptic writers suggest that Jesus's period of teaching lasted no more than a year, the crucifixion might be thought to have taken place in AD 30. But the John gospel again confuses the issue by suggesting that Jesus's ministry was of not one but three years' duration, leaving us sure of nothing.

So given all these problems, and the findings of many biblical scholars that the gospels are not quite the contemporary, direct eyewitness documents that many Christians assume, how can we be sure that Jesus even existed? It is often remarked that Jesus is independently referred to by the Roman writers Tacitus and Suetonius but these references are in fact worth very little. Describing the burning to death of

some Christians in Rome on the orders of the emperor Nero
(54–68 AD), Tacitus remarked that the Christians' "origin-
ator, Christ, had been executed in Tiberius's reign by the
governor of Judaea, Pontius Pilate." Writing of a Jewish
insurrection in Rome in the reign of the emperor Claudius
(41–54 AD), Suetonius described this as at the instigation of
one "Chrestus". Since both Tacitus and Suetonius wrote in
the early years of the second century AD, both were
considerably removed both in time and place from any
original Jesus. So is there any other source of corroboration
to which we can turn?

In fact there is, in the works of the already mentioned
Jewish writer Josephus who was governor of Galilee within a
generation of Jesus's death. According to Josephus's writings
in "Antiquities":

> "At about this time lived Jesus, a wise man, if indeed one
> might call him a man. For he was one who accomplished
> surprising feats and was a teacher of such people as are
> eager for novelties. He won over many of the Jews and
> many of the Greeks. He was the Messiah. When Pilate,
> upon an indictment brought by the principal men among
> us, condemned him to the cross, those who had loved him
> from the very first did not cease to be attached to him. On
> the third day he appeared to them restored to life, for the
> holy prophets had foretold this and myriads of other
> marvels concerning him. And the tribe of the Christians,
> so-called after him, has to this day still not disappeared."

Now as already remarked, since the rest of Josephus's
extensive surviving writings show that he was a loyal
Pharisaic Jew, and quite definitely not a Christian, most
scholars have very justifiably recognized this passage as an
interpolation by some much later Christian copyist of the
Josephus manuscript. For instance, it would be quite out of
character for Josephus to have called Jesus "the Messiah",
and in fact in a later passage in "Antiquities", a reference to
Jesus's brother James, Josephus describes him as "the brother
of Jesus *called* the Christ" (i.e. the Messiah), which is much
more what we would expect. But, as has recently been

recognized by Jewish scholars, the two Josephus passages taken together show that Josephus must originally have said *something* about Jesus. This is corroborated by the third century writer Origen who happens to have noted with surprise that although Josephus spoke warmly about Jesus's brother James, he did not acknowledge Jesus as Messiah. This shows that the manuscript of Josephus's works which Origen consulted must have contained the remark about James, but could not have contained the sentence "He was the Messiah". And some of the first passage's phraseology used of Jesus – "a wise man", "one who accomplished surprising feats" – while quite uncharacteristic of any Christian writer, is typical of what we would expect from the genuine Josephus.

The logical inference is that we are dealing with a passage which has been tampered with by some Christian scribe, but is not a complete invention. So is it possible to get back to what Josephus originally said about Jesus? As it happens, this might still survive in a version of Josephus's text quoted in a tenth century universal history by an Arabic historian called Agapius. This reads:

"At this time there was a wise man who was called Jesus. And his conduct was good, and [he] was known to be virtuous. And many people from among the Jews and the other nations became his disciples. Pilate condemned him to be crucified and to die. And those who had become his disciples did not abandon his discipleship. They reported that he had appeared to them three days after his crucifixion and that he was alive; accordingly, he was perhaps the Messiah concerning whom the prophets have recounted wonders."

As can be seen, all that happened to Josephus's original passage was that a Christian scribe made a few unethical enhancements, but he did not totally invent it. Josephus quite clearly both knew of and wrote of Jesus. So in blunt contradiction of Professor Wells's arguments, we have testimony of Jesus's existence from a Jew who, as governor of Galilee within a generation of the time of Pontius Pilate, must have rubbed shoulders with individuals who had actually known Jesus as a flesh-and-blood human being.

Nor is this our only reason for believing there was a genuine, historical Jesus. Despite Lord Dacre's assertion that there is no evidence for Jesus's existence dating from earlier than the fourth century AD, the facts are that there are some eighty earlier scraps of Christian gospels, the most notable being a fragment of the gospel of John, found in Egypt, and dating from the early second century AD. This is today housed in the John Rylands Library, Manchester. Although these fragments do not themselves bear the actual dates when they were written, their genuine antiquity can be reliably determined from matching their handwriting characteristics with those of other, non-Christian documents of known date. Since the John gospel is generally thought to have been the last to have been written, and the John Rylands fragment was copied from some earlier document sometime between AD 100 and 125, it is reasonable to assume that all four canonical gospels had been committed to writing within, at the outside, three generations of the time of the living Jesus.

And when we study the gospels themselves they give us further reason to believe that they record the words and actions of a genuine flesh-and-blood individual. Most notable in this respect are the parables and sayings, which even the most iconoclastic and hard-headed of biblical scholars generally acknowledge have, by their very nature, suffered the least tampering and adulteration through second and third-hand transmission. Of particular importance and fascination is the imagery. Within a single chapter of the Luke gospel Jesus is conveyed as knowing how to revive a barren fig tree, sensitive to farm animals' need for watering, aware of the remarkable growth propensity of mustard seed, well informed on the amount of yeast needed to leaven dough, and keenly observant of the characteristic way in which a hen gathers her brood under her wings.

It is quite clear that we are dealing with a man whose heart lay, not in any town, but in the countryside, Galilee having been a particularly fertile agricultural region back in the first century AD.

Nor do the parables derive from any dull and sterile set of

rules of life. Each is an individual story with an artistry all of its own. Not only are the characters most scrupulously observed, as if from real life – the good Samaritan, the prodigal son, the vineyard labourers, and many more – each story almost invariably has an unexpected, Agatha Christie-like twist, with honest sinners, rather than the self-righteous, often turning out to be the heroes. It would have needed a singularly brave and brilliantly perceptive mind to author such individualistic mini-sagas, and if that mind was not of the man we have come to know as Jesus of Nazareth, we would need to look for someone else equally remarkable.

So we may be confident that there really was a genuine historical Jesus, and even if the gospels are not necessarily as first-hand and infallible as some like to believe, nonetheless they deserve to be treated with far more respect than they have received from the likes of Professor G.A. Wells. For instance while the John gospel, with the long speeches it attributes to Jesus, has long caused biblical scholars serious problems in harmonizing it with the rest, it also happens to provide such a detailed and geographically accurate account of Jesus's last hours in Jerusalem that there seems little doubt that it contains, in part at least, some first-hand eyewitness material, an overturning of the view of many German biblical scholars of a century ago.

But if it is accepted that there was a flesh and blood historical Jesus who walked the by-ways of Galilee and Jerusalem two thousand years ago, why should we necessarily believe, as Christians are required to, that he was rather more than just an ordinary man?

In "Jesus: The Evidence" I confined myself very narrowly to the strict hard evidence. In doing so I questioned rigorously the evidential basis for the gospels, offering an objective appraisal of the known facts. Many people were astonished that a practising Roman Catholic could adopt such an approach, but my conscience is clear.

We live in a harshly realistic twentieth-century world, and if the best of contemporary scholarship shows that there are flaws, discrepancies and weak elements in the Christian gospels, then I believe it entirely wrong for the intelligent Christian to bury his head in the sand and pretend these do not exist. If it is possible to show that there are at least glimmerings of contemporary parallels to Jesus's healings and exorcisms in the work of modern hypnotherapists and faith healers, then I contend we should consider these without prejudice in the hope they may teach us something about those acts of Jesus that have previously been labelled 'miracles'. It may be a leaner, but nonetheless healthier faith if some of its more mythological accretions are tossed aside.

But in any case there is no reason why the contribution of contemporary science and scholarship should necessarily be all destructive. Thanks to relatively recent documentary and archaeological discoveries, the historical setting in which a historical Jesus would have moved is now vastly better understood. A monument with Pontius Pilate's name has been found at Caesarea. The fine homes of the Temple's Sadducean aristocracy have been excavated. It is possible to reconstruct with some clarity the seething political stage of Jewish-Roman in-fighting on to which Jesus so fatally moved. And in its own way this reveals that special something quite unearthly about Jesus. In his response to every situation Jesus can be seen to have acted, and to have required others to act, entirely without concern for self. John the Baptist had asked for the man with two cloaks to give away one to the man who had none. Jesus asked him to give away both. Previous Jewish prophets had asked their listeners to love their neighbours. Jesus asked them to love their enemies. The consistent code of conduct urged by Jesus was for the turning of the second cheek, for the going of the second mile, for forgiveness not merely seven times, nor even seventy times, but seven times seventy times – in other words, to infinity. In all sorts of situations, such as in the payment of the vineyard workers, Jesus seemed to go beyond normal human justice to something much, much deeper.

A first crucial observation is that such ideas genuinely reached beyond anything anyone had contemplated before – and remain uncomfortable even for the most committed Christians to this very day. Jesus had, as it were, stepped out of time. A second is that Jewish scripture had promised the coming of a very special prophet/king, the Messiah, or anointed one. And it is quite evident from Matthew that while Jesus may not have openly declared himself as Messiah, he quite unequivocally saw himself in this role.

Now Jesus was not the only Jew to have proclaimed himself, tacitly or otherwise, as his people's Messiah. As but one example, this was done a hundred years after his time by the guerilla leader Simon Bar-Kokhba with an equally fatal outcome. But while other Messiahs saw their role as would-be political liberators, and for many Jews this was what the Messiah was intended for, Jesus interpreted the scriptures in a quite different way. Not for him the glory and self-satisfaction of even the most transient military coup. As is quite clear from his parable of the wicked husbandmen, he saw himself as victim of those who were using God's house – i.e. the Jerusalem Temple – for their own ends. And in effect he programmed himself to die at their hands in a classic demonstration of the ultimate in self-surrender. While in doing so it is quite obvious he betrayed human feelings – the Luke gospel in particular lays stress on the mental anguish he went through during the time he awaited arrest – it is equally obvious that he hoped for no earthly rewards. When we put together Jesus's now certain flesh-and-blood existence, his extraordinary teachings, his equally extraordinary works of healing, and this utter selflessness with which he knowingly took on an excruciating death – a death which would breed as many Christians as the bloodcells which poured from him – it is difficult for even the most hardened sceptic not to notice something a little unearthly about Jesus. Was he simply out of his mind, as even his family were wont to think in his lifetime? Or was he out of this world?

This is an aspect of Jesus that by its very nature goes beyond anything that can be offered as hard evidence, and the non-Christian sceptic might well feel it demands a faith that he finds in all honesty beyond what he can muster. It is a predicament with which I can readily sympathise, since as an ex-Doubting Thomas it was my own religious viewpoint until, by the most imperceptible process, I moved from agnosticism to a very liberal-minded Catholicism fourteen years ago.

But for me there has been an extra element, in its own way another item of material evidence – quite literally so – but in another sense also quite other-worldly; I refer to the Turin Shroud, the fourteen foot length of linen cloth preserved in Turin Cathedral. It is a subject I have quite deliberately avoided including in the normal run of evidence for Jesus because it has itself yet to be proved genuine, something that may never even be possible. The crucial feature of the Shroud is that it appears to be imprinted with shadowy stains which when seen in negative reveal themselves as a photographic image of Jesus's body as it would have appeared when laid out for burial two thousand years ago. The first reaction is of course to scoff. The Middle Ages were notorious for forgeries of religious relics, and the Shroud must be one of these. One critic remarked his surprise that one who took so critical a stance towards the historical and documentary evidence for Jesus should be so gullible as to believe in the Turin Shroud. However, I believe the Shroud to be genuine precisely because I have pitted my every critical faculty against it, and it has emerged unscathed every time.

The point to the Shroud is that it is not an item of evidence that one can beat around the head of the unbeliever. The Shroud is essentially something passive. You have to come to it. Very eminent pathologists, past and present, have studied the apparent wounds it shows and have convinced themselves that these are genuinely what one would expect from someone crowned with thorns, scourged, crucified, and speared in the chest in the manner recorded of the gospel Jesus. Criminologists have studied the botanical debris, such as pollens, in the Shroud's dust, and have convinced themselves that it has genuinely spent part of its history in Israel and other regions of the Near East. Chemists and microanalysts have studied its stains and satisifed themselves that these cannot be the work of any artist. My task was to try to reconstruct where the Shroud might have been before the Middle Ages, and I satisfied myself, beyond my wildest expectations, that the Shroud could be historically traced even in the earliest centuries, arguments I set down eight years ago in my book "The Turin Shroud".

For the genuine searcher for evidence of Jesus, the Shroud is therefore something which can be approached in an unashamedly questioning and open-minded spirit. No-one, not even the Roman Catholic Church, demands belief in it. But once it is even begun to be studied, the Shroud raises quarrels in the mind all of its own. As it begins to seem impossible that the extraordinary 'negative' image could be the work of a forger, equally it becomes evident that it is not what one might expect to be produced on a grave-wrapping by a normal dead body, however sweat and blood-stained. In normal circumstances an imprint could be created only by those parts of the body which had been in direct contact with the linen, the rest remaining unaffected, and images created in this way, whether seen in positive or negative, are invariably grotesque and without any of the 'photographic' qualities evident on the Shroud. The uniqueness of the Shroud image is that it contains subtle gradations of tone, in photographic parlance half-tones, representative of those parts of the body which were not in direct contact with the linen, but nevertheless affected it in a way proportionate to their distance from it. The implications are profound. For the Shroud is either the work of some super-forger, working at least as early as the Middle Ages, who somehow anticipated the invention of photography and has managed to fool a remarkable cross-section of present-day specialists. Or it is a genuine crucifixion victim's grave-wrapping to which something quite remarkable has happened. Was the image somehow flashed onto the cloth by Jesus's dead body? Does it provide us with a literal snap-shot of that still so enigmatic moment Christians call the resurrection?

While that alone would be quite mind-boggling enough, the added feature of the Shroud is that if it is genuine it has somehow survived through two thousand years. There is nothing impossible about this; there are Egyptian linens twice as old, still in remarkably good condition. But given the vicissitudes of Christian history, and what I have come to understand of the Shroud's earlier history – even in 1532, when it was nearly destroyed in a chapel fire, the scorches and burns somehow missed the all-important image – the Shroud gives one the uncanny impression that it has been intended to survive to our own time. Could it be by a mere accident that this should be the very time in which we make so many demands for material evidence? Could it be mere coincidence that ours should be the age in which, uniquely, we have the technology at least to begin to understand something of the Shroud's secrets? In other words, could the Shroud have been intended to survive for the Doubting Thomases of the twentieth-century?

As already remarked, it is most important that the Shroud should not, of itself, be considered evidence for Jesus. But for those who seek this, and who have satisfied themselves from other points of view that there was a genuine flesh-and-blood Jesus who walked in Galilee two thousand years ago, it offers a unique extra focus of inquiry and meditation. In no other object can be found the same combination of human image and glimpse, however hypothetical, of the moment when Jesus became more than a man . . . .

KEITH WARD

Keith Ward is Professor of the History and Philosophy of Religion at the University of London. He studied philosophy at Cardiff and Oxford before teaching logic at Glasgow University. In 1970, as a complete atheist, he wrote a highly detached book entitled, "The Concept of God" which sceptically examined the philosophical meaning of the word 'God'. In the intervening years he has become a committed Christian who occupies a fairly traditional position within the Church of England.

In his most recent books "Holding Fast to God: A Reply to Don Cupitt" and "The Battle for the Soul" he argues that Christianity has nothing to fear from the world of philosophy and that belief in God is entirely consistent with our understanding of the world.

The Step of Faith

"I believe because it's absurd". So wrote Tertullian, an early Christian theologian. And, taken out of context, this just about sums up what many people think about Christian belief. It's absurd; it cannot be justified by reason; it goes totally beyond the evidence and anyone who accepts it is making a sort of blind leap into the dark. People will often say, 'Oh, that's only a matter of faith', as though that puts it entirely beyond rational discussion. Now I have been a professional teacher of philosophy in British universities for twenty years. My job is to use reason ruthlessly and relentlessly, to criticise all beliefs and opinions and subject them to strict rational analysis. So obviously I do not have much sympathy with the opinion that faith is absurd. But it may well be asked how I can be both a philosopher, committed to pressing reason to the extreme, and a priest of the Christian Church at the same time.

I must begin by admitting that I once thought it was impossible. Modern philosophy in the West since at least the time of Rene Descartes, has often recommended doubting everything. Descartes' most famous statement, "I think, therefore I am" was his almost despairing attempt at finding something that was beyond doubt, when, everything else, even the whole world itself, could be seen as illusion. Yet Christian faith seems to require absolute commitment, and commitment to a lot of things which are disputed by highly intelligent people – things like the existence of God, life after death, miracles and the unique status of an ancient Palestinian Jewish prophet. When I started teaching philosophy, I invariably criticised all such religious claims, and, despite an interest in religion, I could not really see how a rational person could believe so many very odd things on so little evidence.

Over the years, however, I began to be very dissatisfied with what I was doing. I had assembled a marvellous array of acute analytical tools which could effectively dissect and demolish almost any positive statement that anybody ever made – except perhaps the most trivial ones like 'There is a table in front of me now'. As a matter of fact, I could even do a fairly good job of demolishing that one, too. For those were the days when Positivism still flourished in the land and Positivists analysed things like tables into sets of purely private sense-data which were not enduring material objects at all. I believe that the sort of philosophy I was teaching was a most valuable form of intellectual discipline. It forced people to think hard about what they were saying and about the reasons they could give for their views. It forced them to be precise, articulate and clear. But it was, it seems to me now, essentially a methodology, a way of thinking, and had nothing positive to say about either the nature of the world in which we live or the major moral problems which we face. In fact, philosophers in those days went out of their way to deny that they could tell us any truths about the world or solve any of our moral problems. I well remember Professor Gilbert Ryle, my tutor, who wrote one of the most influential books of the time, "The Concept of Mind", saying that he knew nothing about psychology and did not consider such knowledge relevant in writing a philosophical book about mind. For he was assembling and analysing some of the concepts we use in ordinary speech and no technical knowledge was required.

The beginning of my conversion to Christian belief was, I suppose, the growing feeling that philosophers should have something to say about the world, about the way things are, including issues such as abortion, euthanasia and nuclear deterrence. Wasn't it some sort of denial of intellectual responsibility to say that we were just analysing the meanings of words while all around us great ideologies and moralities surged and competed for dominance? And then I began to see the limitations even of the methodology we were using. Anyone who has studied formal logic in any depth soon realises that the more strictly defined and formally elegant your logical system is, the less it corresponds to the things that people actually say all the time. In logic, there is a widely accepted theorem, Gödel's theorem, which entails that no system of logic can be proved to be both consistent and complete. And there is a wider generalisation of this theorem which might be put like this: consistency is bought at the price of comprehensiveness. I can put the point even more briefly: logic corrupts.

Now of course that epigram needs to be treated with some care. Logic does matter enormously and we go around uttering contradictions at our peril. It is important to find out if our arguments are valid and our conclusions properly established. Where logic can corrupt, however, is when we insist on trying to put everything into a precisely defined set of propositions, from which we deduce a set of clear conclusions. This can give rise to a totally misleading idea of reason. It can lead us to think that a rational person is one who starts from a set of certain and clearly defined premisses and argues deductively from them to his conclusions.

But that is not what rational behaviour is at all. It is, indeed, an exercise of reason to put things clearly and to deduce correctly. That is a rational activity. But it is far from being the only one.

If we say somebody is reasonable, we more often mean that he is good at perceiving correspondences or resemblances between things others might not have noticed; that he is a good judge of the strength or weight of arguments; that he is good at assessing the relevance of various data and in seeing when a topic has been adequately dealt with: good at discerning patterns and connections among phenomena. Rationality is, in other words, a skill which lies in a certain sort of perception, insight, ordering and balancing of things. Logic only corrupts when the passion for clear definition and deductive forms of reasoning lead us to forget these wider factors of rational activity; when our urge for system and precision leads us to falsify the nature of the subjects we are dealing with and to impose a misleading model upon them.

What has all this got to do with faith? Well, the point is this. I came to think that my view of reason had put a two-fold blinker on my perception of things. First, I treated reason as an almost wholly critical and destructive instrument for exposing incoherencies and fallacies of argument. Second, I treated rationality as a matter of setting out clear and precise definitions and sticking strictly to valid deductions from them, not saying anything that didn't fit into such a system. In opposition to these views, I came to feel that reason has also a positive function which is, not to destroy, but to understand the very many and very varied sorts of things that people say and believe, involving not only the study of concepts on a page but the study of the forms of life within which certain sorts of beliefs make sense to people. And secondly, I came to feel that it was not the job of reason to impose formally deductive systems onto the world but rather to understand the complexity, haziness and manifoldness of that world and of our ways of understanding it. In other words, reason should discern the limitations of its formal systems as well as their merits.

And in all this, I was repeating in my own way the great transformation that had come over the work of the philosopher Wittgenstein between the writing of the "Tractatus Logico-Philosophicus" and his later writings like the "Philosophical Investigations". At first he had wished to construct a logically perfect language in which everything would be clear and precise so that "Everything that can be said, can be said clearly". But then he came to see that this was both impossible and undesirable. The world is much too complicated to impose any neat and simple logical scheme on it. The ways we understand the world are subtle and complex, and they require much more careful and sensitive ways of thinking if they are to be at all adequate to the way things are.

In that vastly over-simplified first stage, you could get rid of God, faith and religion just by saying that they did not fit into your neat scheme. But when you get to the second stage, you see that what is wrong is your scheme. It is too simple and indeed it probably cannot be defended from criticism itself. Positivism vanished as quickly as it appeared, under a deluge of trenchant criticism. It was not replaced by a new and equally simple system. Rather, it was replaced by an attempt to understand the subtlety and complexity of human thought, belief and the language in which this is expressed.

The brief flurry of Positivism had done some good. It did make quite clear that whatever religious talk of God and the soul was doing, it was not just stating a set of supernatural facts – things just like physical facts but thinner or more ethereal. In other words, it got rid of a lot of superstition and woolly-mindedness. But then when you begin seriously to ask what the concept of God really means, you are introduced to some of the hardest and most fascinating of all philosophical problems. If theologians speak of God as eternal and infinite, self-existent and necessary, what are they saying and how does it make sense? The old Positivist response would have been to say, 'Oh, it's all rubbish, nonsense; ignore it'. But when you consider that almost every philosopher in history whom we would call great has given serious consideration to problems of time and eternity, finitude and infinity, necessity and contigency, it begins to seem facile to dismiss them. We have to make an effort to understand them, to understand how they were used and what their role was in the lives of those who did use them.

When you see this, the way is opened to a proper understanding of belief in God, and it is no accident that so many of the pupils of Wittgenstein are Christian believers. What we have to get rid of is the idea that the world consists of a list of clear and precise facts and that when we have completed such a list, we will have understood how the world is. If you think like that, then arguments about God become arguments about whether there is an extra item on the list called God and if so, whether you can prove that there is. So you begin to talk about proofs of God, and you get side-tracked into fruitless disputes about how you can prove God, or whether you just have to believe he is there by some sort of irrational leap of faith.

Whereas the situation is not like that at all; and, until we get perverted by misleading philosophy, none of us thinks it is like that. We do not go around the world making lists of the things that exist and then try to construct some sort of proof that there must be a God on the list, even though he is peculiarly hard to find. Faith is not about the hidden extra ingredient; and all of us know that intellectual arguments about God somehow miss out the most important point. And that is because religious faith is, or is founded upon, a certain form of insight, a way of seeing how things are, a way of living in and reacting to the world, a vision of ourselves and of our total environment.

Let me try to make a parallel with the existence of other people. There is an old philosophical puzzle about how we can know that any minds other than our own exist. After all, we experience our own thoughts and feelings but we never experience the thoughts and feelings of others in the same way. So, philosophers have said, we can never be really sure anybody else is having any feelings at all. Maybe they are just responding to stimuli, without any real feelings. And if this sounds odd, remember that it has been seriously said about frogs, beetles and even dogs and cats. How, then, do we know anybody else ever has feelings?

Well, one sort of argument goes, we have to observe their behaviour and then say that it is very like ours and infer that, since we have feelings, they must be having them too. This is an argument from analogy; we infer that other people have feelings by a rational argument, even though it is a bit of a leap of faith. Now I do not wish to explore this argument further; that would take a course in philosophy. But I do suggest that we all know something has gone wrong here because we do not in fact have to infer that our parents and children have feelings; we jolly well know that they do and if any philosophical argument seems to disprove it, the so much the worse for the argument. How do we know they have feelings? It is in fact almost impossible to say. But the fact is that we begin our lives by interacting with other people, by responding to them, by being taught by them, by just assuming that they are persons with whom we have a living relationship. It is a given datum of experience. Any formal logical system which denies that is inadequate to the facts. And maybe we cannot find a formal system rich enough to convey precisely what we know but cannot put into words. Personal relationship is a form of life which helps to define what we are; it is a framework within which we live. Reason can neither prove nor demolish it. Reason can only hope to articulate it, make it clearer, draw out its implications or destroy misleading accounts of it.

Now I suggest that something the same is true of faith in God. We know that people do not believe or disbelieve in

God because they have gone through some set of arguments or assembled the right sort of evidence. Belief in God is a form of life which helps to define what people are, something which sets a framework for their apprehension of and reaction to the world. Again, it is a datum of experience for those who have it. That is what is wrong with trying to isolate special moments called 'experiences of God', since all life is lived in the presence of God. Reason cannot prove or disprove this form of life but it can draw out some of its implications or destroy misleading accounts of it, trying to make clearer just what its character is – though always tentatively and sensitively, not in the superior dismissive tone of the Positivists.

What I am saying is that faith is not a leap beyond reason. It is a particular form of life, a way of seeing the world, within which reason has a proper place in seeking to order, clarify and explicate. But of course the chief problem with all this is that not everybody believes in God. We all believe in other people and their feelings, so we can accept this as a basic form of life, beyond proof or disproof. But we know that not everyone believes in God; so maybe this cannot be a basic form of life after all. Not only that, but there are very good reasons for not believing in God – the existence of vast and terrible suffering counts against the existence of a loving God and maybe the laws of physics simply leave no room for a God to operate, so that he becomes irrelevant. At any rate, it is perfectly rational not to believe in God so this can hardly be a basic belief.

I quite agree that for people living in a twentieth-century Western society, belief in God is an option, not an assumption. So you have to ask what is involved in that option. That brings me back to my feeling as a philosopher that I was not standing for anything. I was not engaging in the most important arguments of the time. I could criticise anything but say nothing, and my particular philosophical technique was somehow limiting and restricting my vision rather than widening and extending it. As I thought more about it, it came to seem that part of what it is to be human today is to be forced to choose the basic options by which we live. We are not in a society where we can just go along with the general stream and accept our beliefs as given, beyond reflection and criticism. And at this point the philosophers of Existentialism – Heidegger, Sartre, Marcel, Jaspers and Kierkegaard, spoke strongly to me. They emphasised that to be human is to choose, and to choose authentically, on behalf of humanity, accepting responsibility for what one is to be. They stressed that this will be a practical choice, a choice of a way of life. In a world which does seem ambiguous, we have fundamental choices to make which will govern what our lives become. We can choose the pursuit of wealth; we can choose sensuality; we can choose commitment to a political or moral cause.

Not only can we choose. We cannot avoid the choice since even doing nothing is a choice of inaction when we could have done otherwise. There is no escaping the risk and the commitment of choice. We choose what our lives will become in the uncertainty from which none of us can escape, and yet in a moment of commitment which is in practice final and decisive. And it is important to see that this choice is not merely or simply a moral choice, a choice about principles on which to act. It presses even deeper, to become a choice about how we see ourselves and our world, not just a choice about what we shall do, but a choice about what we shall be and thus about what we truly are. At this level, the practical and the theoretical overlap and conjoin and cannot be clearly disentangled. Thus, I might choose to pursue wealth because I believe that I am a doomed organism in a purposeless universe, and so I should enjoy what I can while I can. But has that view of myself itself been influenced by my inclination to seek wealth above all? Are my theoretical vision of the way things are and my practical decision about how to act quite separate? Or are they not rather interwoven in an inextricable way?

Now it may seem strange to say that we can choose how we see the world; for surely we cannot help how we see things. We must simply seek to see them as they truly are. It is strange, perhaps, yet choice is involved in our most basic perceptions. Even at the level of everyday perception, we choose to attend to certain things and ignore others. We focus our interest on certain aspects of the world and this in turn affects the way we tend to see the world more generally. It is no accident, for instance, that lawyers, whose interest is in finding rules and analogies, attending to precedents and judgements, tend to be conservative and legalistic in their general religious and moral views. The general point is that though we cannot choose what world we perceive, choice enters at many levels, largely unnoticed, into the way we see that world and how we interpret it.

Now the religious vision is a combination of a way of seeing the world and a commitment to a course of action within it. It is the point at which the most basic perspective on the world and the most basic form of practical commitment merge. So, for example, a Buddhist might see the world as a realm of suffering and dissatisfaction. That is how he truly sees things yet it is clearly an interpretation which others do disagree about. It is not a vision of how things truly are but a personal vision which is affected by basic commitments and predispositions. Then the Buddhist will commit himself to a life of meditation and the renunciation of passion and desire. And again that is a practical commitment, made because it seems appropriate to the world and not chosen by arbitrary decision but in response to a factual assessment. Here we can glimpse the way in which factual interpretation and practical commitment interact in subtle ways, ways which are unique in each individual case.

What then is the vision and the choice which underlies Christian faith? Well, in each case it may be unique but there are general factors we can pick out. I think the vision would be that the world, at its deepest level, has a personal and relational character. That is, as we go through our daily experience, we are in relation to a total environment which expresses rationality, purpose, meaning and value, in and through which there is a presence best described as personal or like that experienced in human interpersonal relationships. It is important to preserve the sense of the mystery and otherness of God for we are not talking about a particular object within the universe. We are trying to express something about the character of the universe as a whole. And we are using analogies from human relationships to point to something about this universe which makes it appropriate to speak of us facing moral demands, promptings and feelings, of peace and strengthening and visions of hope and courage which seem to come from outside ourselves and to be expressed through the world that environs us. That is the theoretical part, a vision of the personalness of things at their deepest level of being, a sense perhaps that the material is the vehicle and sacrament of the spiritual but not the ultimate and sole determining reality.

What of the practical commitment? At least in the Christian faith, this is a commitment to love; a commitment which needs to be spelt out by reference to the vision of God seen in the person of Jesus Christ. Christian love is a response to God's love; it is a love which sees all people as in God's image and, in that derived sense, as holy; which sees every human life as having a hope and a destiny of fulfilment; which sees commitments of fidelity and honesty as absolutely demanding. It would, in my view, miss the point completely to say that we can commit ourselves to love of our neighbours, without any reference to God. For the commitment to such love springs from and is intertwined with a response to the vision of God's love on the cross of Christ. That is what defines its character, its origin and its goal. It cannot be spelt out in a set of principles but only in the story of a life, the life of Jesus, seen as expressing the character of God which is the personal basis of the cosmos.

Let me try to sketch the position as I saw it those few years ago. I had to decide how my life would go, what it would express or stand for. And I felt that I could not just divorce the practical commitment from the theoretical side of how I saw the world. One had to be a response to or expression of the other; they had to cohere, in quite a tight way. I was never attracted to Camus' apparent path of total moral commitment in a world of uselessness and despair. My practical commitment had to be a rational response to how the world was, while at the same time I was aware that how I saw the world would partly be a function of my hidden commitment.

Seeing the necessity of some sort of worthwhile commitment, I realised I had no commitment. I had the endemic disease of all intellectuals, being paralysed by an excess of rationality. Yet the answer was not to renounce reason. It

75

was rather to use reason to recognise its own limits; to see that I had to take the risk of commitment in a world where nothing would ever be certain.

It was at that stage that revelation came into the picture for me. And this is where one can properly speak of something like a 'step of faith'. At this point I find the analogy of marriage quite helpful. You might decide you would like to get married but you are not sure to whom. There are a number of possible candidates, none of them, if you are ruthlessly honest, absolutely perfect. So you make a list of their plus and minus points but something is still missing. It is a very rational thing to do, but there are limits to it and a marriage-partner may well feel aggrieved at being told he or she scored best on the compatability test. No, if you're lucky, what might happen is that one of these unfortunate people may in some quite mysterious way come to insinuate themselves into your consciousness, to upset all your calculations and take the choice out of your hands altogether. In a phrase, you fall in love. You are totally captivated. What can you say? You might say that you see something in that person which you cannot put into words but which shows them to you as quite special. It's been a revelation. They have shown you something about themselves that you might well have missed, that you hope most other people do miss, maybe, but which transforms your vision of them and your feelings towards them. They have reached out and touched your heart and you'll never be the same again. Now you might still get cold feet before the wedding and run away. Or your love may unfortunately cool and you may begin to look in other directions. You don't have to take the step of faith which is involved in committing yourself until death to another person with all its attendant risk and uncertainty. But if you do take that step, it's not just a one-way decision. It's a whole-hearted response, made in faith, to something that has come from outside you and changed you and that will go on changing you as you continue responding to it in fidelity throughout your life.

Again, the sceptic may say that marriage-partners do actually exist; you can see and touch them, fortunately. But the trouble with God is that we aren't sure whether or not he exists at all and here the analogy, touching though it may be, breaks down. That is quite true. But the point is that we do not have to try and guess whether or not God exists through pure thought. The Christian Church claims that God has revealed himself in history and invites us to respond to him. When you trace this claim, you find that it appeals to a long line of prophets who claimed to be inspired by God to declare his will. They claim, not that they were necessarily deep thinkers, but that God took them by the scruff of the neck and spoke through them by the inspiration of the Spirit. Then it appeals to the testimony of the apostles that they had seen their teacher Jesus raised from death; and he had commissioned them to form a new community, the Church, wherein he would be personally present to the end of time. And it appeals to the testimony of members of that Church throughout two thousand years and continuing today, that they know and feel that Jesus the Christ lives and is present in their lives in a transforming experience of re-birth and renewal.

What can a philosopher do with such claims? I cannot say they are impossible or self-contradictory. In fact, once I conceive the possibility that the cosmos may have a personal basis, that it may have a meaning and purpose that I am meant to commit myself to, then it becomes quite probable that such a God would in some way declare that purpose. Once I see the possibility of God and feel the necessity of practical commitment, then it is only rational to be on the lookout for writings or events which may reveal his will and purpose. Now this does not eliminate the ambiguity and uncertainty of God. But remember that God is not an object in the world. The world itself does exist and our problem is to say what its essential character is: whether it shows meaning, value and personal presence or not. It is a problem of how we interpret it adequately. And this is where revelation claims to show, reveal or disclose the essential character of the world, its origin and basis in a personal will.

In this light, I believe it's entirely rational to respect the integrity, wisdom and intelligence of those who convey the alleged revelation; to try the experiment of response, to taste and see how good the Lord is. The step of faith is a sort of response, experimental at first maybe, to the vision of a personal God which the Church proclaims as its good news to human beings. I can only record that when I did that, I found a transformation of life which can only be described as like falling in love with a personal reality which showed itself in and through the world and in particular in the person of Jesus. Or perhaps it would be better to say it was like being grasped by a love which drew me up into itself from beyond my own resources.

Philosophers are human; they do not have access to secrets that other people know nothing about. They should have a greater knowledge of the sorts of reflection on human life and the world which the greatest and most reflective thinkers in human history have produced. I would say that most philosophers have always taken as a central part of their concern the problem of God and the character of ultimate reality. They have rarely been entirely orthodox because they are keen to press their own original insights and arguments. They have often pressed their own favourite theory so far that it forces the world into a conceptual strait-jacket. This happened with Positivism early in this century. But at its best, philosophy extends the mind and enriches the possibilities of understanding. Many strands of argument suggest a rational or personal basis to the world – the intelligibility of nature, the demands of morality and the mystery of existence itself. But there are difficulties too – how can a good God cause suffering? How can such a God act in what may seem an impersonal cosmos? Philosophy will not resolve these issues. But it will force us to face the mystery and tragedy of human existence and show the fragility of human systems of thought as well as the necessity of practical commitment without final answers.

If that is what philosophy does, then it is in no way incompatible with faith. We must reject the misleading picture that rational people only believe what the evidence compels them to believe whereas religious believers go leaping in the dark. For the hard questions are about what is to count as evidence, what commitments one should make, how to interpret the world of human experience and how to understand one's own being. From the Christian point of view, this quest for understanding is guided and enlarged by God's revelation of himself in Christ. For there, the truth which we seek shows itself or opens itself to our gaze. If we see reason as the attempt at an adequate, enquiring response to what is disclosed to us of reality, then it is no longer opposed to revelation but it is drawn to its full and proper activity by revelation. So, rather than follow Tertullian, we might rather say, 'I believe, because it increases understanding and sets it on its proper task'. Is that, after all, saying so much more than that reason can tell us about the world because the world is open to reason? Understanding discloses the nature of reality to us because that reality opens itself to our understanding. Perhaps, then, revelation is already implicit in our attempts to use reason to understand nature. Faith and reason are not opposed. To think that the world is rational is already one step of faith. It is another step to respond to that world as personal but it is not a step beyond reason. It may be a step which opens up to human reason and understanding the true depth and riches of the character of ultimate being.

DAVID JENKINS

David Jenkins has been the Bishop of Durham since 1984. He became a household name on the eve of his consecration when he expressed severe doubts about the truth of the virgin birth and Jesus's resurrection. In his first year at Durham he made numerous interventions during the British miner's strike, enraging government ministers with his outspoken views.

After leaving the army at the end of the last war, he studied philosophy and theology at Oxford, going on to teach at Queen's College for 15 years. He subsequently worked for the World Council of Churches in Geneva for which he travelled throughout the world, developing an interest in liberation theology and Marxism. He returned to England to become director of the William Temple Foundation, a radical organisation which looks at the Church and society. His most recent book is "The Contradiction of Christianity."

Re-searching the Question of God

Christianity is not primarily about what we may, can or must believe about Jesus. Christianity, at its heart, as a living faith rather than a religion or cult, is about what Jesus is about – God. This God is to be believed in and responded to as the ultimate reality who is the creative possibilities within all present realities and the promise of a final reconciliation between facts (what is) and value (what is worthwhile). Ultimate reality, therefore, is to be thought of and worshipped as love and glory, holiness, justice and truth. Once we return centrally and persistently to the question of God then we shall get all our debates, difficulties and differences about the truth of Christianity, the source of its authority and its future into a lively and creative perspective and dynamic.

This will turn Christian discussion and exploration outward into a pilgrimage, open to all men and women, and into a mission to share in the searching for a God who repeatedly finds us and sends us again on our way. We shall be wrestling not with idle questions of religion or atheism but with vital questions of reality and our response to it which are pressing and practical in the lives of all.

To illustrate what it means to focus on the question of God and respond to this reality I will attempt to explain why I find myself obliged to claim that I am claimed by God and how this relates to other human attempts to get to grips with the world such as science, politics and sheer down-to-earth commonsense about the taken-for-granted ordinary. Shortage of space obliges me to tell a story rather than develop an extended argument but I hope the direction along which the argument proceeds is sufficiently apparent.

My recollected awareness of a claim about God which had to be taken seriously starts from a simple evangelical experience of a type which is well known and well documented. In the language of those who seek to live for such experiences I was 'converted.' In the following exposition I do not attempt an account of either the cause or content of this or subsequent experiences. I am simply trying to convey what I now make of them or what they now make of me.

The significance of my conversion experience centres around three things. The first is a proclamation of 'Jesus is Lord'. The act of proclaiming something meant that here were a group of people who were on to something and were concerned to help other people to get on to it. The proclamation was of something received and this conviction defined the group. The slogan 'Jesus is Lord' pointed to the nature of the discovery or reality they claimed to be on to. I call it a slogan not in order to trivialise it but to indicate that its use and implicit meanings are very complex and that it served as a rallying cry and symbol.

For me, what the slogan now seems to have indicated is a claim for the central importance of Jesus. Whatever it is about Jesus that one ought to know, this was central to what everything is all about and what is on offer to me and all men. 'Jesus is Lord' meant and still means that Jesus is somehow the expression of that which has a decisive claim on my sense of reality and should have on all men.

Of course, initially the claim was not seen in that abstract sense but in a rather specific one which is related to the other two important features of my conversion. The first is a sense that 'this will make a lasting difference'. I am reflecting here on what in the technical theological language would be called 'encounter'. Certainly I recollect a sense of being up against something about which something had to be done because it was there and was something one could count on. The evidence for this lies in a feeling that despite extreme and erratically episodic fluctuations this was a real sense that has never left me and has been frequently renewed.

The other more precise content of that experience is expressed in the notion that 'Jesus died for me'. There was quite a theory put out about this, explaining that Jesus died for my sins and for all men and that by his death we were put right before God. While I was intellectually interested in this theory and particularly the biblical evidence for it, it was not the theory which impressed, attracted or even troubled me too much. What did impress, attract and trouble me was the 'for me'.

I was clearly aware that there was a claim on me which arose out of something which had been done for me and was offered to me; something which called for my commitment. So I found myself caught up in a community which proclaimed 'Jesus is Lord' and thereby caught up in a process of an offer which called for a response.

This process I felt to be a very serious business, a business which promised to make all the difference in the world. I have been pursuing and pursued by this 'difference' ever since – and this pursuit remains the central purpose and promise of living.

In case I am being too allusive let me point out that I am trying to give an evocative account of what I find believing in God to be like and why I am compelled to hold that this is a source of experiences which makes serious claims on my sense of reality. I have begun with a brief autobiographical narrative for several reasons. While one gets on to believing in God in a communal context it necessarily involves personal encounter and commitment. Further, one can point to what is meant by 'being up against' or 'getting to grips with' through a narrative of faith. Thirdly, I am thus describing one possible entry-point into the coming-alive of the Christian traditions about God.

What I am attempting to do is to evoke a sense of the reality claims which are involved in the tradition of which my experiences have made me a part. This claim insists that it ought to be the strongest of reality claims and in the end will be. What has been decisively exciting for me has been the expansion of the reality claim which I have encountered 'through Jesus' in the direction of infinity, eternity, transcendence, holiness and all of humanity.

The impact of the proclamation 'Jesus is Lord' upon me was to persuade me that I should take God seriously. Thus God became a power, a possibility and a presence with whom I could have dealings and with whom I should have dealings. Prayer became a possible practice and worship opened up as an activity which was both welcome and necessary. Self-conscious awareness of God seems to have started from the consciousness, to which I have already referred, of the presence and the possibility who was 'for me', of that which was going to make so significant a difference, of that which was both pursuing and to be pursued. God thus began to emerge, as far as I am concerned, as the reality within all realities and beyond all realities who is to be responded to and explored.

In all this there is an interaction between the stories about God which I am picking up from the bible and from the community who proclaim to me Jesus as Lord, and the shaping of my own experiences. By the 'shaping of my own experiences' I mean both the active way in which my own experiences of dependence, difference and pursuit help to give form, content and force to what the stories about God mean to me, as well as the passive ways in which these stories inform and feed my experiences. I am not able to separate my being told about God from my finding out about God and the totality of this continuing and immensely unfinished process is, I think, better described as my being found by God. It is a process very much bound up with, although not confined to, a community and a tradition, and this community and tradition has a lot so say and to offer about what is involved in 'taking God seriously'. In entering into all this I have found myself moved on from the compelling slogan 'Jesus is Lord' to the central mystery of the Thrice Holy.

One of the best known focusing and crystallising points in the tradition and experience of this mystery is to be found in the call-vision of the prophet Isaiah:—

"In the year of King Uzziah's death I saw the Lord seated on a throne, high and exalted, and the skirt of his robe filled the temple. About him were attendant seraphim, and each had six wings; one pair covered his face and one pair his feet, and one pair was spread in flight. They were calling to one another,
Holy, holy, holy is the Lord of Hosts:
The whole earth is full of his glory."

The translators of the Authorised Version suggested that the last line might be better read "his glory is the fullness of the whole earth."

Thus the coming alive of an experience of the worshipful God is a discovery about the possibilities of everything. But this is not the primary discovery. The primary discovery is the discovery of the existence of glory. Our intimations of value, of worthwhileness, of immense wonder, have a focus which is at once their ultimate source and their final fulfilment, while at the same time being beyond and going beyond anything we have dreamed of or glimpsed. The difference which the 'for me' promises to make is an infinite field of energy and value which is immensely beyond me, intimately associated with me and offered to me as an exploration and an interest without end. But the difference which is proffered and promised already exists in its completeness and is to be worshipped. This 'to be worshipped' does not get its compulsion from an anthropomorphically mistaken notion of some celestial tyrant who egoistically requires the recognition of his greatness. It is simply the demand to share in the sharing, to give to the giving and to glory in the glory. When one can finally praise, then one will be part of the total contribution to the praiseworthiness of everything.

The worship of the Thrice-Holy God through Jesus and in the Spirit is a celebration of, a contemplation of, an awareness of and a waiting for, a presence who is also an absence and a promise. This trio of sets of experiences of presence, absence and promise which are sustained and fed by a community and a tradition points towards a living and energetic source of inexhaustible claims on our sense of reality and the shaping of ourselves and our world. Thus the mystery who is worshipful is no encouragement to mystification and muddle. Quite the contrary. The glory of God demands and authorises the most ruthless and rigorous engagement with all lesser realities in their own proper authenticity, autonomy and hardness.

This is made particularly clear by the connection between the glory of God and people. This connection was not an obvious or conscious part of my initial and initiating experiences of faith. It is only gradually that I have experienced what I have described as "the expansion of the reality claim which I encounter 'through Jesus' or 'in the name of Jesus' in the direction . . . of all humanity".

The discovery has come about in the process of an attempt (which still continues) to be realistic about love. It is as difficult to write about this as it is to write about worship and the glory of God. No doubt the basic reason for this is that love and glory are one and the same in the energy and being of the ultimate mystery which will fulfill us beyond our most sober, and our most extravagant, imaginings. However, the more immediate and practical reasons lie in the very slight knowledge and experience I have of these matters, and, most particularly, in the extremely inadequate ways in which I have so far responded even to such knowledge and experience as I have. Nonetheless, a persistent falling short in a realistic response to realities glimpsed or engaged with does not diminish the power of these realities. It increases the longing for an adequate response to, and realisation of, what is glimpsed and tasted. It diminishes only the power to bear witness to the reality. I hope, therefore, that what I have just written will not be read as an expression of that contrived modesty which is really conceit, nor of that type of excuse for poor performance which is really laziness.

In all probability there are traces at least of both these failings. But the statements just made are necessary as part of an attempt to be realistic about experience and knowledge which has to do with the realities of which I am writing. It would be wholly unrealistic to claim any experience, knowledge or response which is in any way adequate to them. This, however, is a measure, not of the depths of despair, but of the extent of hope. For the glory and the love, while they reveal the depth of our inadequacies and shortcomings, are at the same time experienced as energies at work to bring us into a full participation in what is glimpsed. Thus, the difference which is to be made is that of overcoming what is now the gap between what we are and what we need to be, so that we can enjoy, and contribute to, the full glory of God. The pursuit in which we are engaged is precisely the response to the one who, or the power which, is pursuing us, so that the mutual pursuit can come to its fitting fulfilment.

Thus inadequacy for the reality is no bar to attempting to point to the reality nor any discouragement from continuing the attempt to pursue and respond to the reality. I may continue therefore with my endeavour to explain the developments arising from an attempt to be realistic about love. To be offered a glimpse of a God who is loving and glorious is to be invited out of myself. It is to make the discovery that the possibilties for myself lie beyond myself and to begin to entertain the notion that fulfilment lies in everyone and in everything else. But this is not a contradiction or an overwhelming of myself. It is a promised transformation and consummation of self. So, in the depths of my being and at the heights of my longings, the two commandments cease to be commands. I am not commanded to love God and my neighbour. This is what I most want to do. It is clear that the whole of my life and, indeed, of all life, lies in the discovering, the learning, the applying and the enjoying of such love. But what is the relation between such a glimpsed, promised and compelling reality and the realities of other people, of myself, and of the ordinariness of which I and everyone else are a part?

I have found that the immediate effect of being faced by this last question is that my attention has been directed towards people in a new way. This new way has not involved my seeing them immediately or directly as "in the image of God", or "all persons of infinite worth because we are all loved by God", or "all equal as individuals in the sight of God" or of the other phrases by which insights from the Christian tradition are customarily turned into statements about people.

What I have found is that I have been required to give serious attention to what is to be seen in the faces and in the situations of my fellow men and women, with as much clarity as possible and with as much understanding as possible of how they see themselves and their situations. That is to say that I have been re-directed to the reality of people. This has meant being re-directed to people as a source of pressure upon my sense of reality. Claims about either the nature of God or the nature of the universe, the direction of history or the essence of politics, which ignore or distort what people are really like are essentially unrealistic and must be combatted as such. In facing up to and seeking to respond to reality people have to be reckoned with.

As I have said, this obligation and desire to take people seriously in and as themselves fitted in with a discovery of the reality of God. But the point that now needs to be made is this. Once people are attended to in this way it becomes clear that you do not need God or any particular theory about the relationship between God and people to justify taking people seriously. People constitute, in their own right, a claim upon one, upon one's sense of value and upon one's sense of reality. An essential part of being human, once one has been alerted to it, is a passion for people.

This is as much a discovery in its own way as the discovery through Jesus that God is for me and the subsequent discovery of the worshipfulness of God. Attention to human faces; to what they reflect, reveal or conceal; to how they attract, repel, cause interest or threaten boredom; to the interactions they display and the threats and promises which they offer; all this becomes something you must give, something you want to give or at least something which will not leave you alone. Supposing people actually matter ('really' matter!) as much as they seem to matter, as much as I seem to matter to me and to those who love me, as much as those whom I love seem to matter? This emerges as a compelling question which becomes a matter for persistent exploration. Thus people are discovered to constitute a vast and vital field of demand, of offer and of mutual pursuit. But this discovery about people is not a smooth one. Concern for people has to face turbulence, contradiction and anguish. There is so much human waste both exacted from people and inflicted by people. So much behaviour seems to be impelled by aggressive negativity and by stupid and callous self-centredness, while one is acutely aware oneself of how attitudes and conduct are constantly making nonsense of one's own visions, concerns and commitments. All this threatening evil and pain is quite as real as the enjoyment achieved, the glory glimpsed and the excitements promised. Passion for people thus forces us into an engagement with realities and a search for possibilities of response which will measure up to both the threats and the promises of what has so far been experienced. This sort of sensitivity to our common humanity constitutes an autonomous but interlocking part of the pressures of reality upon us. Whatever may be the pressures of scientific, sociological or political realism upon us and whether or not God is a living possibility to us, this passion for people constitutes an independent demand and pressure upon our sense of reality with which we must reckon.

The demands and offers of such a passion for people are very like the demands and offers of the glory of God. If there were not independent evidence for, and experience of, God in his glory then this would be only a manner of speaking, a metaphorical way of expressing the supremacy and ultimacy of the value experienced in a passion for people. But, as I have been arguing, this discovery of a passion for people fits into a narrative of faith. My glimpses of the glory of God reinforce the passion for people and my passion for people reinforces the search for and response to the glory of God. This encourages the hope and, indeed, develops the conviction, that ultimately the glory of God and the passion for people fuse together in one energy, enjoyment and fulfilment. That is to say that God is love. But that conviction is not an abstraction which diverts us from the particularities of what is happening to people but an insight which can only compel us to a search for realism now.

It is in this connection that it is so important to be clear that people as they are and in their own right constitute a commanding claim and a demanding pressure on our sense of reality, our perception and value and our hope of life. Men and women are not the functions of any theory or doctrine or even vision, however heavenly. They are the subjects and objects of life. Thus, it may be true (and I believe it is) that a very valuable and important way of pointing to what is involved in human potentiality is to speak of us as being in the image of God. But it is hopelessly unrealistic to use this phrase to force interpretations on to the actual splendours, perversities, wickednesses and frustrations of ourselves and our neighbours. If we in any way believe that Jesus is somehow an actual historical embodiment of a fusion of the glory of God and a passion for people then to be a disciple of his cannot involve a wrapping up and avoiding of realities. It must involve facing them and suffering them. (That is to say

90

'experiencing them'. Passion involves discovery and joy as well as lostness and pain). To discover the meaning and reality of any insight of faith such as that of men and women being in the image of God, we have to engage in sustained and corporate attempts to face reality under the pressures of the glory of God, the passion for people and the following of Jesus.

It is necessary, however, to be quite clear about what is involved in 'sustained attempts to face reality'. I am particularly concerned with re-searching the question of God in such a way that we can see believing as essentially an engagement with reality rather than a veneer which we cast over reality or a phantasy by which we escape reality. Thus, what I have been trying to do by this narrative of my personal meaning and experience of Christian faith is to build up a picture of the types of pressures, experiences and demands which constitute the dynamic pattern of faith, of believing in God, of being aware that one is claimed by God. I am clear that the possibilities of belief in God and the particular possibilities of entry into that belief which are focused in the things concerning Jesus must be considered in constant interaction with all the reality claims which confront us. This linking of the question of God with all the other questions about how to get to grips with the world, how we understand other people and about what seems to us to be real, compelling and hopeful or hopeless is a necessity for a set of reasons in which cultural, personal and theological consider-ations interlock.

Culturally it is plain nonsense to suppose that we can forget, ignore or obliterate the insights, developments and achievements of science, the Enlightenment, Freud, Marx and so on. Of course, we must look for the revival and rebirth of those other human cultures which have, until recently, been subordinated to and trampled on by Western expansionism. We may expect therefore some return to ways of looking at the world which are less dominated by science and tech-nology. And of course we must fight the growing tendencies to idolatry, absolutism and dogmatism which are to be seen in attitudes to everything from science to Marxism. That is why a new search into the question of God is so humanly necessary, provided that we have grounds for holding that

God is a reality. But there can be no retreat to a way of looking at ourselves and at the world which is unaffected by all that which has produced 'modernity'. It is not in the first place a question of some simple-minded view of progress, nor of what is good and what is bad, but simply of taking seriously what has happened. A central part of this is the establishment of a critical approach to the world and to the realities experienced in the world.

Further, I am quite clear that it would be humanly disastrous to attempt to go back on, or to attempt to ignore, the achievements and the characteristics of the modern secular mind. On the one hand, the development of radical criticism, questioning and experiment, together with all that has been achieved by this, is a major glory and distinctiveness of the human spirit. That man can split the atom, crack the genetic code and call into question every single thing about society, morals or belief is one of the most powerful indications of what it is to be human. On the other hand, radical criticism, questioning and experiment is desperately needed. The capacity to deceive, manipulate, be content with the unacceptable and to submit to the most absurd and destructive superstitions seems to be the other side of the powers inherent in being human. So to run away from the tools of scepticism which have been so painfully and carefully forged to challenge all this would be to surrender to that side of us which is always betraying us.

Finally, what I see as a human being is reinforced by what I apprehend as a believer. Being 'in the image of God', human beings have immense potentialities and corresponding responsibilities. The abuse of these powers and the betrayal of these responsibilities constitute the problems of hell and absurdity. But there is nothing in the biblical tradition which justifies the denigration of man. What the tradition points to is the necessity of judgement and the need for redemption. Again, a tradition of encounter and discovery which uses symbols and stories about creation, incarnation and bodily resurrection requires us to take any procedures (like sciences, critical history or social sciences) which treat matter and process seriously with an equivalent seriousness. The tradition forbids us to absolutise any such procedures and obliges us to fight the idolising of them, but it does not authorise us to treat the abuses of these procedures as an excuse for rejecting or ignoring what their uses have achieved.

Thus, the pressures on our sense of reality must include the pressure of critical realism alongside the pressures of following Jesus, of worshipping the Thrice-Holy God and of a passion for people. My understanding is that all of these sets of experiences or sources of discovery have to be taken seriously in their own right and authenticity. All are claims on our discovery of reality and our sense of reality, claims which have to be taken into account both in themselves and as they interact with one another. The worship of God *promises* finality and ultimate unity but this is not yet given to us; it is certainly not yet our possession. Therefore our present apprehension of the worshipful must be no more absolutised than the best sense we can at present make of secular reality or the best understanding we can so far have of what will fulfil the passion for people. Discipleship, the responding to God, must consist in a search for consistency, the persistent pursuit of a consistent realism.

Let me now summarise my understanding of God (the 'theology') in a way which indicates the pattern of discipleship which the response to God requires.

The central issue of all is the issue of God and reality. To discover God is to discover that God is ultimate reality, the source of reality, the fulfilment of reality, the value of reality. But we are involved in realities of their own sort and our own sort. To respond to God therefore is to go into, and to get to grips with, these realities in the most serious ways we have of doing this. This involves taking as seriously as we can those methods of analytical and radical assessment of realities which have developed through science, philosophy and criticism, often into conclusions of atheism. It involves also going as far as we can into a passionate concern for people which develops into the openness of suffering love. It involves, further, being drawn as far as possible into the worship of God through and in connection with Jesus, which draws us towards the openness of an encounter in which nothing can be hidden and which will offer its own determination of reality.

Our problem, which is our tragedy, our absurdity or simply our condition, is that the reality of the worshipful God, the realities of the human beings who justify and demand a passionate concern, and the realities of the autonomous processes of matter and energy do not come together. There is contradiction and confusion, waste and wickedness, at least as much muddle as mystery.

But the discovery which constitutes Christians as believers struggling with a realistic way of life rather than a group of people maintaining a religious cult is that Jesus, in his living, his dying, and his living beyond that living and dying, somehow puts us on to the knowledge and experience that God is precisely involved in overcoming the contradictions and obstacles and in bringing the realities together. (One way of putting this is that "God was in Christ, reconciling the world unto himself").

So to follow God through Jesus in the Spirit we must go deeper and deeper into the realities which constitute, determine and distort us in order to discover, through them, the God who will free, enlarge and fulfil us. It thus becomes clear that the hardness and nakedness which dealing with realities requires is the hardness and nakedness of love. Worship of God, and that love of God and men which worship informs and fulfils, demand rigour, analysis and openess to all claims to reality which are prima facie credible or authentic.

Christian discipleship and Christian faith cannot therefore be confined to, or confined by, anxious debates about how the symbols, formulae and doctrines through which the Faith has been expressed, pointed to, are now to be taken in some unchanged and always received sense. Faith and discipleship are about an ever-expanding exploration in response to, and in search of, the dynamic mystery of God. The universality of God is to be experienced in, and worked out through, the experience and expression of faith and in relation to our daily and human lives. But always we are to go further, probe more deeply and move beyond what we have so far seen, grasped or believed. God is always more, always ahead and always more all-embracing than we have yet realised. Faith therefore is a gift but it is not a possession. It is a being claimed by God but it can make no final claims to have got hold of God. It is a journey by those who have an assurance that they are in the Way but can make no fully definitive statements about what is the end of the Way. So we question because of our faith in him who answers us, we doubt because of our glimpse of him who calls in question the adequacy of all our knowing and we search because we have been found, and hope to be found, by the Love that has risked the universe.

JOHN BARTER

John Barter is Vicar of Holy Trinity church in Hounslow in Middlesex where he has created a large, vibrant community which attracts people from many miles away. He strongly believes that God intervenes in the lives of his followers and, in particular, that he wants Christians to enjoy the charismatic gifts of healing and speaking in tongues which the New Testament speaks of.

He has developed a powerful healing ministry at Holy Trinity – from personal counselling to praying for God's miraculous activity – which has witnessed dramatic events over the past decade.

A God who Answers
Prayer

In 1974 my life was transformed. I began to experience for the first time the love of God in action, in ways which you read about in the New Testament.

As a result I have come to see the bible not just as a record of the past but as a certain promise about God's activity in the present. The bible has become for me an exciting and challenging witness to God's purpose for his Church and the world today.

The transformation began with an Easter Monday mission and a rejoicing in the reality of faith, both in the promises of God and in the power of prayer.

At the Feast of Pentecost we prayed that our Lord Jesus Christ would pour down the gift of his Holy Spirit as he had done nearly 2,000 years before on the first Whit Sunday in Jerusalem. Within days we found that the members of the congregation became dramatically filled with the Holy Spirit, so that they found the love of God flooding into their lives and their prayers becoming answered.

In September I began to experience the healing touch of Jesus which truly transformed my ministry. One afternoon I was sitting quietly in my study praying for my wife when there were a couple of 'clonks' in my back. At first, I thought I had put my disc out but when I stood up there was no pain, only warmth in my back and chest. My chest felt very odd for the rest of the day and when it came to go to bed I discovered that my chest, which had always been deeply indented, was now quite normal. In fact, it was three inches larger than before and no longer deformed.

I soon discovered that our Lord had laid his hands on my chest and healed me of life-long asthma. For the first time in 44 years I was free of medication and could breathe freely.

Every time I breathed I was reminded that if he had healed me, he could do the same for those with whom I prayed. And my wife and I decided to share the miracle with our congregation.

We held our first healing service at the church in January 1975 and what happened that night caused our faith to increase even more dramatically.

Halfway through the sermon, which was based on the promise of Jesus that "whatever you ask in my name you will receive", a member of our congregation who was sitting in the front of the church collapsed. There was no escape for me, or for the rest of the church. Either the promises of Jesus were true, or they were not. The music group began to sing and we went to where the woman was now lying stretched out on the pew. A nurse from West Middlesex Hospital told me that she was dead. She had no pulse and she was not breathing, but the moment we stretched out our hands on her and began to pray, she closed her staring eyes, her pulse returned and she began to breathe. Within a moment she was sitting up and asking that she might make her confession and begin her life all over again. As I write this now, nearly twelve years later, she is an active member of our congregation and she delights to tell of the wonderful way in which our Lord ministered to her on that night and gave her a new beginning.

Later in the service when we invited any who were sick to come forward for prayer, the first to come forward was a young boy of seven. He had a severe congenital heart condition and was regularly attending Great Ormond Street Hospital, and his future was very bleak. I asked him what he wanted Jesus to do for him and he said that he wanted Jesus to heal his heart. As we prayed for him, many of the congregation saw the light of the glory of God shine in the sanctuary. Six months later they could find no defect in his heart at all. He was completely healed and later played football for Middlesex Schools and passed with flying colours into the Hendon Police College where his athletic prowess was very soon recognised.

Since that time, thousands of people have come to Holy Trinity for prayer and for healing of all manner of sickness and disease. A great many of them came for the healing of emotional problems; the depressed, the suicidal, the rejected, the fearful, the anxious. We have seen our Lord heal the deep wounds which were inflicted on them as children and bring them into wholeness and newness of life. We have seen people healed of cancer, of broken bones, of kidney disease, and many have been delivered from the powers of evil.

They have come in their thousands over these past ten years to receive new life in Jesus and baptism in the Holy Spirit, to seek prayer for their friends or their family, for their jobs or homes, for husbands or wives, and time and time again we have seen Jesus answer those prayers in a dramatic way. Sometimes we have had to wait to see the answer but our assurance is that the promises of our Lord are there as firmly as they were on that day when he raised the lady from the dead at our first Healing Service.

In a recent survey of our congregation, we found that 27% of those who now worship with us had never been to church before. That means that they have come into the life of the Church without any previous experience of Church membership and have found in Jesus the new life for which they were seeking. They have found Jesus to be for them their Lord, their Saviour and their friend. They know the power of prayer in their own lives, and have a living faith and trust in him and that has brought love, joy and hope to them and to their families.

A church where the congregation expects prayer to be answered is very different from one where there is simply a formal attendance because they feel it is their duty. Our experience of Jesus as being alive, active and present with us throughout our life, as being faithful to his promises, and forgiving and loving in his attitude towards us, brings about in us a response of love and trust, not only towards him, but towards each other.

When in your own life you experience the very things that you read about in the New Testament, you find that you are able to believe what you read, not simply because it is in the bible, but because your own experience is a witness to the truth.

That experience of God's love in action prompts us to ask 'Why should God heal me?' Why indeed? Was it because I deserved it, or was it because I asked for it? In fact, I know it was for neither of these reasons. Like everyone else I am a sinner and do not deserve the goodness of God, but in his love for us, he is willing to give us what we need, even though we can never deserve it.

In fact, it is the very nature of God to love and to give. He does not wait until we deserve his love. He loved us before ever we were born. He gave us his Son, Jesus, to live and to die for us, even though we were sinners. In fact, it is because we are sinners and do not deserve his gift of life that he sent Jesus to rescue us and save us, so that we could become righteous, not through our own efforts, but by being granted forgiveness through Jesus Christ.

Salvation has to do with wholeness, and while the purpose of God, our Father, is that every one of us should find eternal life through Jesus Christ, he is not only concerned with our soul. Throughout the ministry of Jesus we find him healing the sick and preaching the good news of the Kingdom of God. Whenever he came across a person who was in pain or suffering in some way, he stretched out his hand to heal. *Not because they deserved it, but because they needed it.* The compassion of Jesus moved him to heal the sick. It was that same compassion that moved him to preach to the multitudes. Jesus was concerned with the whole person – with their spiritual, emotional and physical life, as well as their relationships with one another.

Jesus said "I have come that you may have life in all its fullness". That promise is not only for life in heaven after you die. It is a promise for a full life here and now. A life that has the quality of eternity about it. A life that is totally different from that which so many people now live. It is a life in which we see love, joy, peace, fulfilment, patience, faithfulness, mercy and hope.

If there are things in our life that make it difficult or even impossible for us to experience that full life, then we know it is God's will to change us or change the circumstances of our life, so that we can begin to live in abundance the life that he has given.

Time and again we see that fact demonstrated in the ministry of Jesus. Before he ascended into heaven he told us that "as the Father has sent me, so send I you". Therefore, it is the task of the Church to continue the ministry of Jesus. To

101

bring to men and women, young and old alike, the healing power of Jesus, to change and transform their lives so that they may be able to experience abundant life.

The Church exercises this extension of the ministry of Jesus by his authority and by his power. I have of myself nothing to give to other people. I am a frail human being, just as they are. However, God has called me to follow in the footsteps of Jesus to continue his work. We have the authority of Christ to exercise that ministry which is recognised and acknowledged by the Church through the sacrament of ordination.

But authority alone is not sufficient. We need to minister in the power of God himself. It is the promise of Jesus that after his ascension, he would send his Holy Spirit upon his Church, and on the day of Pentecost the Spirit of God descended like a mighty wind and like tongues of fire upon the gathering, and they began to minister in the power of the Holy Spirit. They healed the sick, they raised the dead, they delivered those possessed by evil and preached the gospel of God's love. Things have not changed! That which Jesus did, the apostles did, and that which the apostles did, we see today! God is the same. He intervenes in the lives of ordinary people to bring healing and life in answer to prayer and the ministry of his Church.

When we come to pray we are often very anxious about a particular problem and, as far as we can see, we have only one way out. Indeed, sometimes we see no way out and the situation appears to be hopeless. It is this hopeless situation that often drives us, as a last resort, to prayer and that makes us feel guilty, but the fact is that God really does love us. He is not going to ignore us, just because we may have ignored him. But we must realise that he sees our life differently. He knows what would be best for us in a way we can never know. Sometimes we do not ask for the most obvious things because we believe them to be impossible. But, with God, all things are possible. After all, he did create the universe. He did give us life. He does love us. He is willing to forgive us and there is nothing he would not do for us, and there is nothing he cannot do for us.

Sometimes we see only the superficial problem, or the physical problem, or the financial problem that affects our lives, but God knows everything about us. He knows exactly what has caused the problem, how to correct it, and what would be best. Therefore, we have to learn to bring our problems to our Lord in prayer, trusting him to deal with them.

It is right to ask him for what seems to us to be the need, but if he answers in another way first, it is always for our good. For example, when the paralysed man was brought to Jesus, all the people standing by expected him to heal him physically. But Jesus knew that in that particular case the man was feeling guilty, so, first, he forgave him his sin, and then, later, he was able to get up and walk. Sometimes we too find that when we come to Jesus in prayer he deals with something we never thought was important, and yet he knows that until that is dealt with the physical healing cannot come.

In the New Testament we find Jesus saying "your faith has made you whole". To have faith is to trust. Our Lord expects us to trust that he will keep his promises to us and that he will hear and act in answer to our prayer. So, then we pray, we ask that he might give us what he has promised. Then, we must trust him that he has both heard and answered our prayer. Then, we begin to act as if we have received what we have asked for, even if at that moment there is nothing to show for it. That is what is meant by the prayer of faith.

When the paralysed man on the bed was let down through the roof into the presence of Jesus and our Lord forgave him his sin, he said to him "Get up and walk". Now, many people would say, 'How can I? I am paralysed'. But it was in trusting Jesus that he began to get up and as he began to respond so the healing came. In just the same way, Jesus said to the ten lepers "Go and show yourselves to the priests" and, as they went, they were healed. The healing came in acting in trust.

So often when we pray we ask Jesus for something and then say to ourselves or to someone else 'Well, I don't expect it will make any difference, but it was worth a try'. That is not prayer and there is no answer in heaven for that kind of request! Therefore, when we pray we have to trust that our Lord will do whatever is necessary for us, however impossible it may seem. But if he can raise the dead, heal the sick, deliver the oppressed, find a husband, find a job, or find a house in answer to our prayers, he is certainly able to intervene in your life as well and give you whatever it is that you need so that you can live your life to the full.

Someone is bound to say 'Yes, but what do I do when I've really prayed and nothing happens?' Well, I don't believe that nothing does happen. At least, in my experience, something always does happen in answer to prayer. Sometimes it is not exactly what we expected, sometimes not exactly what we wanted, but it is always for our good. Jesus said "If you being evil know how to give good gifts to your children, how much more will your heavenly Father give good things to those who ask him".

In these past twelve years when so much of our ministry has been concerned with praying with people, there have been many lessons that we have had to learn.

When at first we found that our Lord dramatically answered our prayers, we began to expect that all that was necessary was for us to lay our hands on those who were sick, pray for them, and they would go away healed. Indeed, they did, in large numbers, but, gradually, we became conscious that one or two were not healed when first we prayed with them.

On one occasion, we were presented with a case of kidney failure in our congregation. The more we prayed with her, the worse she seemed to get. She was in considerable pain and in and out of hospital. First one kidney failed and she then developed a tumour on the other, and after weeks of prayer she went for a final set of X-rays before seeing a specialist who was going to decide on some radical solution. When he saw those final X-rays, the kidneys were clear and whole. We had learnt our second lesson in prayer; that we had to persevere as well as to trust. It proved to be a most wonderful witness to the doctors and a great encouragement to us. So now when we pray, if we do not see at once the answer to our prayer, we remember that example and continue to persevere and trust, knowing that God's will is to save and to make whole.

We have had another member of our congregation who was deeply depressed, so much so that she was suicidal. On one occasion she visited us at the vicarage and ran out determined to drive her car into the oncoming traffic. There was nothing we could do but to pray for her as she ran out through the door. Immediately our Lord answered. Her car refused to start! Later, after she had allowed us to pray with her, her car started perfectly and she was able to drive home safely, but for years she continued to be depressed and in a very sorry state. During all this time, our Lord gave us a continuing love for her. No matter what she said, or what she did, our Lord sustained our love for her and, eventually, the day came when she came to know the wonder of God's love for her, that he loved her for herself and that she was precious in his eyes. In the eight years that we prayed with her and for her, our Lord had answered by giving us a gift of love for her and gradually as she came to experience that unconditional love on a human level, she was able to experience it in her relationship with God.

That was not the way we expected to see the answer to our prayers, but the joy that we all experienced together when finally she was healed was simply wonderful. We had learnt another important lesson; that God is building a community of people here on earth to be a loving, caring community, which is, in itself, a part of the healing that he longs to give to all mankind.

Then there was a young mother who died of cancer. At the onset of her illness she was not very deeply involved with the life of the Church, and she probably had a fairly nominal faith. However, after she discovered that she had cancer and we started to visit her and to pray with her, there was a remarkable change. Not in her physical condition, because she still had cancer, but in her spirit. Throughout her illness in hospital and later in a hospice, she had no pain. She was not on any kind of painkiller and gradually she became more and more conscious of the presence of Jesus. When I saw her shortly before she died, she said to me "I don't want you to be worried about me, I know that I am with Jesus every moment of day or night. It is so beautiful and I am going to be with him. I know he will look after me and I know he will look after my family".

If only we could all die in such peace and such assurance of the love of God. How can you say our prayers were not answered? True, on that occasion we did not see the physical healing that we longed to see, but we saw a spiritual growth and healing beyond anything that we have ever seen in anyone who has been physically healed!

Since that time we have prayed with many people with cancer and some of them have been physically healed, and we have learnt to continue to trust no matter what we see when first we pray.

Once you discover that God is for real and that his love and power are with you all the time, you find that you turn naturally to prayer. Not just in times of crisis or disaster. It becomes natural to praise him for those things that remind you of him, and to pray for those things that don't.

JOHN HABGOOD

John Habgood has been Archbishop of York since 1983. He is a natural scientist who lectured in physiology and pharmacology at Cambridge before taking orders in 1953. He has held a number of academic posts within theological colleges and is seen as one of the Church of England's leading intellectual figures, being particularly interested in the relationship between religion and science.

He is also actively involved in the debate about the relationship between the Church and society, recently writing "Church and Nation in a Secular Age". During the 1984 miner's strike he invited the leaders of the National Union of Mineworkers to his official residence, Bishopthorpe Palace, for exploratory discussions.

Discovering God in Action

Just before taking part in a CREDO Programme on prayer, providence and miracles, I was told about a certain clergyman who claimed that his prayer for parking spaces in central London was always miraculously answered. His explanation was that God knew he was a bad driver, and therefore took special precautions to get him quickly off the road.

When I publicly expressed some doubts about this story, I was inundated by letters from those who accused me of not believing in prayer at all, asserting its power in their own lives, even in such detailed matters as convenient travelling arrangements. One letter to a newspaper described how the correspondent's car exhaust had become detached on a motorway. He stopped on the hard shoulder to pray about it, and immediately spotted an old rope and a discarded pair of gloves, presumably planted there by God to enable him to do some running repairs. Unfortunately a subsequent correspondent pointed out that tying up exhaust pipes with old rope is one of the easiest ways of starting a fire.

I begin with this story, trivial though it is, because it highlights some of the difficulties in ordinary Christian language about acts of God. On one level it seems natural and obvious to talk about God taking a personal hand in the detailed lives of individuals. The bible is full of such stories. God makes promises and fulfils them. He answers the prayers of the faithful. He is to be found, not just in great events like the Exodus from Egypt, but in feeding a poor widow and her son. Admittedly, some of his actions are puzzling. Why should he harden Pharoah's heart, and then punish him? But that he is active, that his will makes a real difference to what happens, is never questioned.

This certainty is echoed in the lives of many believers. It is true that there are some for whom prayer is mostly a matter of hanging on to faith in God against the evidence of their feelings, and who do not expect to see any miracles. But there are countless others who, in perhaps less bizarre ways than my motorists, would want to point to moments when God has touched their lives with his providential care, and for whom any expression of doubt about his loving personal attention would seem like a denial of their deepest and most precious experiences.

Yet on another level the question, 'What kind of world is it in which God can be said to act in response to individual needs and wishes?' is very puzzling. For the believer, caught up in a relationship with God, there may be no problems. 'Of course God acts in my life. Don't I see signs of his concern for me every moment of the day?' But for the detached observer, trying to reflect on the experience, there are difficulties. Broadly speaking these fall under three heads.

First and most obviously there are difficulties which spring from a scientific understanding of the way things happen. Whatever the limitations of the scientific approach, and they are many, the fact is that it has revealed to us a universe which by and large operates according to fixed rules. There may well be exceptions. There is no need to be old-fashioned determinists and to exclude miracles on *a priori* grounds. Modern scientists, particularly physicists, are a good deal more humble in making claims about what can or cannot happen than some of their predecessors. But a world which lacked a basis of ordered regularity would not only make science impossible, it would make life impossible too. If everything keeps changing, as Alice discovered when trying to play croquet with live hedgehogs and flamingoes, the game dissolves into chaos.

A few exceptions, in other words, can be tolerated within a broad structure of scientific order. But multitudes of special interventions in the regular workings of the universe threaten the whole intellectual edifice which science has created. This is why large miracles are less of a problem than small ones. Large ones are likely to be infrequent and easily identifiable. There is only one resurrection. But miraculously-provided parking spaces for all the bad drivers who want to go to London would seem to reduce the notion of miracle to incoherence.

The second type of difficulty in trying to think rationally

about God's action in the world is internal to theology itself. It focuses on the question of God's normal relationship to his creation. If, as we have seen, the biblical story and much subsequent Christian experience require the use of language about God intervening in the world if they are to be taken seriously, then what is God doing when he is not intervening? The point was made epigrammatically a hundred years ago in early discussions about Darwinism:

> "Those who oppose the doctrine of evolution in defence of a 'continued intervention' of God, seem to have failed to notice that a theory of occasional intervention implies as its correlative a theory of ordinary absence."

The usual theological retort to this is to distinguish between God's general providence, his regular upholding of the order of nature, and his special providence whereby he overrides the order of nature to meet some particular need. But it is a distinction which, if badly presented, can easily lead to the charge of incompetence. If God is constantly having to intervene in order to keep the universe on course, why didn't he make it better in the first place?

This brings me to the third kind of difficulty in conceiving of God's action, and in some ways the greatest problem of all – the moral one. I am not thinking primarily of some of the moral actions said to be commanded by God in the Old Testament. Instructions to slaughter the Amalekites, men, women and children, have to be put in the context of a primitive and very partial understanding of God's will. Nor am I thinking simply of disasters ascribed to the direct action of God, horrific though some of these have been. The famous Lisbon earthquake on All Saints Day, 1755 shattered much eighteenth-century confidence in a beneficent providence, partly by its sheer scale, but more particularly because the greatest sufferers were Christians attending church. Such sufferings, though, are part of the general problem which haunts all belief in the goodness of God, whether he is imagined as actively sending disasters or passively allowing them.

A theory of God's active intervention certainly has a lot to explain, but the <u>difficulty I mainly have in mind focuses on</u> <u>the moral disproportion between different kinds of action</u> <u>and inaction.</u> How do those who claim that God is intervening for them in the trivial affairs of everyday life explain his silence at Auschwitz? No doubt in the fine detail of terrible events there are many hidden examples of people who have been lifted above tragedy, and have found God's sustaining presence in the depths of suffering and degradation. No doubt, too, God's providence is an unfathomable mystery, and it is not for us to judge what is morally appropriate and what is not. But an unbeliever cannot be blamed for wondering why a God who can reserve parking spaces for his chosen ones could not divert a few Nazi death trains.

I have done no more than sketch in barest outline some of the difficulties, scientific, theological and moral, which any belief in God's active and continuous intervention has to meet. Together they add up to a formidable case, yet this has to be set against the experience of many Christian believers that God can indeed be known personally, that miracles do happen, and that prayer is more than whistling in the dark. How can we reconcile these two points of view?

In what follows I want to suggest a way of thinking about <u>God's action which meets at least some of the difficulties.</u> It <u>cannot meet them all because lurking in the background of</u> <u>the discussion is the greatest of all theological problems, the</u> <u>problem of suffering, to which no merely intellectual answer</u> <u>can ever be satisfactory.</u> At the heart of much contemporary unbelief lies puzzlement, to put it mildly, and in the most sensitive people rage and anguish, at a world full of horrors where God seems not to care. Christians would be wise to admit their own puzzlement, and I shall say more about this later. But the essential point to be made at the moment is that the Christian response to such horrors has always been a practical one. God cannot be understood as the direct cause of suffering, but he can be known in the midst of suffering, because he bore the agonizing weight of his own creation on the cross of Christ. Whatever I suffer, says the voice of faith, Christ is beside me. The ultimate end of any argument, therefore, has to be 'Try it and see'. And this sets a limit on how far our intellectual understanding of God's care, and our practical experience of it, can actually be brought into harmony.

With this proviso, I return to my main theme, how to make sense of the notion of God's intervention. And I want to start by drawing a distinction between the notion of 'intervention' and the notion of 'miracle'. They are obviously interrelated, in that both presuppose an unusual occurrence in a normally self-contained process, but the word 'intervention' points to some extraneous cause for the occurrence, whereas 'miracle' describes its effect in evoking wonder and faith. Not all interventions need be regarded as miraculous. It is possible to imagine all sorts of adjustments taking place in a system which occasion no surprise because their true nature is not known. The creation of a work of art may be an intervention in the natural order of things, but we only describe it as a miracle in a metaphorical sense.

Equally it is possible for events to be regarded as miraculous in a certain state of knowledge, but later to be given naturalistic explanations. Healing miracles, for example, even some of those performed by Jesus, may seem less strange as more is known about the complex interactions between mind and body, but may be no less effective in evoking a religious response.

There is a difficulty, though, inherent in both definitions, which centres on the phrase 'a normally self-contained process' against which miracles and interventions have to be judged as such. It is the uncertainty about what this phrase means which can easily make both definitions circular or vacuous.

The classic argument against miracles exploits this circularity. If the so-called laws of nature are based ultimately on what is experienced as happening, so the argument runs, then it is self-contradictory to envisage them being broken. If there are genuinely new and unexplained facts, they always lead eventually to reformulation of the laws. There is therefore no place within science for the concept of miracle. The good scientist remains agnostic about such claims, and waits for the results of further investigation or for the reformulation of fundamental concepts.

Similar logical puzzles arise in relation to the idea of intervention. To provide a context for it I had to refer to the normal process of events as being 'self-contained'. But this, as readers will have spotted, begs the whole question. It seems to presuppose a universe which is only occasionally related to God, whereas Christians have always claimed that the main characteristic of created things is precisely that they are not self-contained; they are dependent at every point on God's sustaining power.

Perhaps we need a different starting-point, one which by-passes these difficulties of definition, and goes straight to what words like 'intervention' and 'miracle', and belief in answered prayer and providence, mean to those who claim to experience them. At their heart we find awareness of God as a loving personal presence. The so-called interventions are the actions of a friend; miracles are his capacity to surprise us; answered prayer and providence are the signs that he hears, knows and cares. The basic analogy, in other words, is not that of a law-giver who can sometimes be persuaded to override his own laws, but that of a person who responds to personal approaches in all the freedom we normally associate with personal action.

Thus the answer to the question of how God acts in the world lies in asking how we as persons act in the world. Though it is hard to describe exactly what we mean by it, most of us assume that by and large we are free agents. What we choose to do actually makes a difference to the way things are. Yet this free action takes place in a world, and through bodies and brains which, despite much about them that remains mysterious, seem to operate in an orderly fashion.

Our own direct experience, therefore, poses problems about the nature of personal action in a law-abiding universe. It would be absurd to have to suppose that we break the laws of nature every time we act freely or create something new. The general and reasonable assumption underlying the scientific investigation of brain processes is that they can eventually be understood in terms of ordinary physics and chemistry. But it would be equally absurd to suppose that when the scientific story is told, that is all there is to say about our experience of thinking and feeling, intending and willing, loving and being loved, in other words about personal action.

Somehow we need to imagine the ordinary processes of nature as being open-textured. The world is law-abiding, but the laws are such that they allow the unexpected and the unpredictable to happen. This is true in the deep interstices of the stuff of which the universe is made, as the physicists have been discovering. It is also true in the most complex structures, of which the human brain is the supreme example, which seem to generate a new dimension of freedom in their mode of operation. Whatever the details of the picture, something of this kind is needed to do justice to the inner conviction of most rational people that there is at least one place in the universe, in our own hearts and wills, where what happens is open to be influenced by personal decision.

Is this best described as an 'intervention' in natural processes? Or does it make more sense to think of natural processes as already containing this possibility of free creative personal action, when the right conditions obtain? I pose the question to make the point that for an adequate description of human personal action, the concept of intervention may not be strictly necessary.

If this is true of us, may it not also be true of God? What I am suggesting is that we should think of God as working through the regularities of nature in the same kind of way that our personhood manifests itself through the workings of our bodies and brains. The parallel is not exact. The universe is not God's body, nor is he dependent on it in the sense in which we are dependent on our physical nature. But if the complex stuff of which we are made can provide the conditions for personal activity, then the physical structures thus opened up for our exercise of freedom, must be equally open to God. As George Macdonald said about prayer:

"I may move my arm as I please: shall God be unable so to move his?"

'Intervention', therefore, is probably the wrong word to describe God's normal mode of action in caring personally for his creation. The alternative is not a mindless universe bound by inflexible laws and set in motion by a remote deity who never actually does anything. The point of my argument has been to suggest that the possibilities of action, both ours and God's, are built into the structure of creation itself. God does not therefore need to intervene because his action is already continuous.

It is useful, though, to distinguish between different types of action, and it is here that the distinction between general and special providence can be restated in a less objectionable way. Austin Farrer once described two kinds of predictability:

"The Parry-Joneses come to call. We rely on Uncle Peter and cousin George to rise to the occasion. There are many things we are sure they will not do. They will not talk across to one another and ignore the Joneses. They will not go on reading Country Life and The Sporting Times. They will not insult the Welsh character. But these are negatives. What will they do? Our reliance on them to act characteristically may involve very different expectations: about Uncle Peter the sickening certainty that he will tell the anecdote of the two Irishmen; about cousin George, that he will sum up his company in the twinkling of an eye, draw them out, pick up the points of their interest, and lead them on into one of those charming conversational games, in the invention of which he has an inexhaustible fertility. In fact, we rely on Uncle Peter to do, alas! exactly what we expect; and with an equal confidence we rely on cousin George to do what we don't expect."

Built into our experience of life are expectations, both positive and negative, providing the secure framework within which alone stable and responsible existence is possible. Science is one means of mapping such expectations. From a theological perspective its laws are the hallmark of the consistency of God's will.

But God, thank God, is more like cousin George than Uncle Peter. He is the source and inspiration of endless creativity. Within a scientific context one of the evidences is the phenomenon of life itself, constantly diversifying in ways which are both ordered and unpredictable. Theologically speaking the consistency of God's will carries within itself the perpetual possibility of surprising us.

Miracles are among God's surprises. Just as unexpected human actions can reveal new depths of character, even when they are later seen to be part of a consistent pattern, so unexpected happenings can be especially significant in revealing God, even if no actual laws of nature are broken. We have already noted the logical difficulty in that last phrase, and it is in avoiding this that the language of 'expectation' and 'surprise' shows its advantages. What counts as a miracle depends in part on what people know. The fact that knowledge and expectations change may mean that an event which was once regarded as a miracle is now seen in a different light, but this is not to devalue it as a genuinely revealing encounter with God. The point is simply that God acts in ways appropriate to those with whom he is dealing, and *autres temps autres moeurs*.

To acknowledge this is not to deny that there are also acts of God which are as surprising and inexplicable now as they were to those who first witnessed them. The miracles of the incarnation and the resurrection are the supreme examples. Though it is possible with hindsight to see even the resurrection as part of a larger pattern, the actual experience of discovering life out of death, hope out of despair, and victory out of defeat, whether in the historical event of Christ's resurrection or in contemporary manifestations of its power, still remains gloriously unexpected. Christians hope *against* hope. Yet such hope is not mere folly, because it is grounded in God's faithful consistency.

There is thus a subtle interplay in Christian experience between ordinary and extraordinary happenings, both of which provide the context for personal relationships with God. In the very nature of things ordinary happenings are likely to be more frequent than extraordinary ones, and I have already expressed my preference for believing in a few big miracles rather than lots of little ones. But, let me repeat, to deny the name 'miracle' to finding a parking space in London is not to deny that there can be genuine thankfulness for answered prayer. The point is that the whole of life can be interpreted as personal encounter with God, because the universe only exists at all as it is held in being by his will. Prayer opens us up to this reality. And because God's action is seen in its most revealing forms in those places where the open texture of the universe is most apparent, in other words in the exercise of human freedom, prayer can also properly be understood as releasing God's power to act, a power which manifests itself most characteristically in and through the actions of people. Prayer stretches the fabric. It enlarges the area of freedom. Indeed at its very heart lies the acknowledgment of our human freedom to ask and to seek and to expose the longings of our hearts, and God's freedom to give or withhold. Any prayer can therefore rightly issue in thankfulness because, whatever the answer in terms of perceived results, the main purpose of exposure to God's loving care has been achieved. George Macdonald again:

> "What if the main object in God's idea of prayer be the supplying of our great, our endless need – the need of himself? . . . Hunger may drive the runaway child home, and he may or may not be fed at once, but he needs his mother more than his dinner."

I hope I have said enough to indicate how the analogy between God's action and our own can begin to meet the first two difficulties, the scientific and the theological ones, in reconciling actual Christian experience with critical reflection. There remains the third difficulty, the moral disproportion between what are claimed to be God's actions and the actual tragedies of life.

I have already made the point that there is no intellectual answer to the problem of suffering. Such answers as have been attempted always come back in the end to an assertion of human freedom, an assertion which, arguing from different premises, I have already made the centrepiece of my account of God's way of acting. Not only does God use the openings in the fabric of the universe provided by the possibilities of human choice; he also respects that choice. At its best this mutual acknowledgement of freedom finds conscious expression in prayer. At its worst it exacts a terrible price in suffering, a price which Christians claim can

117

only be met in and through the sufferings of Christ.

These are deep mysteries of which I am only skirting the edge. But my main concern here and now is not with suffering as such, but with 'disproportion'. If God really counts the hairs of our heads, what was he doing during the Lisbon earthquake? Or even more pointedly, why did he not hear the cries of the victims at Auschwitz? Can the same God personally will empty parking spaces for some lucky clergyman, as well as sudden death for thousands of his worshippers in church on All Saints Day? And what of those millions of Jews slaughtered, not despite their religious allegiance, but because of it?

Such contrasts are not to be explained away by theological sleight-of-hand. Their effect is to make it morally intolerable to describe all events equally as manifestations of God's will. There has to be some principle of selection and interpretation.

I have already indicated one such principle in distinguishing between God's action through human agencies, and his general work in upholding the regularities of nature. Take the regularities first. A universe which is 'open' enough for human freedom to be a reality may have to be unstable enough for calamities to befall it. Such perils as movements of the earth's crust may be part of the price which has to be paid. Earthquakes, in other words, belong within the regularities rather than within the personal and particular manifestations of God's will. This does not imply that they should be dismissed as religiously meaningless, only that their meaning emerges more in the response to them than in the events themselves. If God is chiefly known through personal actions, then personal heroism and self-sacrifice in the face of disaster, the faith which does not give up, the suffering which becomes the ground of compassion, may speak more truly of him than the shuddering of the earth.

But what of his action through human agencies? Here again it needs to be stated firmly that not everything that happens can be directly ascribed to the will of God. Indeed it is basic to a Christian understanding of the world that much of what happens is in flat contradiction to his will. The worst evils derive from sin, and the hard message of the cross is that sin can only be ultimately defeated by suffering love. To ask what God was doing in Auschwitz, therefore, is to invite the reply – 'Suffering with those who suffered.'

The distinctions I have been making entail interpretations of the evidence, which may or may not seem convincing. The point I want to draw from them is that some kind of interpretation is necessary. The nature of God's actions in the world, whether these are seen as active expressions of love or passive permissions to let human freedom do its worst, cannot be deduced solely from the raw evidence. There has to be some general framework of understanding about what kind of acts can properly be described as acts of God. This interpretation is not simply imposed on the facts. It grows out of them and is modified in the light of them, and sometimes has to be drastically revised, as happened more than once in the developing theology of the biblical period. Nor did the process stop with the bible. Though all Christian theology finds its central reference-point in Christ, there has to be a continuing process of dialogue between theological interpretation and actual experience. And elements in this dialogue may be decisively transformed by events of the magnitude of the Holocaust and the Lisbon earthquake.

The essence of the moral objection to the over-easy identification of trivial everyday events with the direct personal intervention of God is that such an interpretation encourages too cosy and narrowly-based a theology. This is not to say that it is wrong to pray about such events and to be thankful for blessings. The hairs of our heads are indeed numbered. But it is important also to be aware of the spiritual perils in believing that the world is especially ordered by God for our own personal benefit. The classic example of such distorted vision is in the traveller's prayer of thankfulness when his seat on the aeroplane which crashed was taken by somebody else. Not to see in the midst of such natural thankfulness that it raises theological problems, is to be blinded by spiritual self-centredness. In other words, a sense of moral disproportion has to play a major part in the interpretation of what are believed to be God's actions. Without it the way is open to moral enormities.

I have argued in this essay that God is seen most clearly and characteristically at work in human lives, especially in the lives of those who freely open themselves to him in prayer. But such an interpretation of human actions and responses needs to rely on a framework of theological understanding which has taken seriously the conflicts and contradictions of actual experience. Above all it needs to be rooted in those central Christian events, the incarnation and the resurrection, in which God's actions were not merely mediated through the channel of human freedom, but encountered directly in a human life. Here is the touchstone. If from this central affirmation a glow spreads over the whole of experience to transform it into loving dialogue with a faithful creator, there can be true spiritual growth. But if the mystery and the majesty, and the wrestling with contra-dictions, are overshadowed by an uncritical and self-indulgent intimacy, then there is an ever-present danger of relapsing into fantasy.

CHRISTIAN BELIEF

PAUL BADHAM

Paul Badham is senior lecturer in Theology and Religious Studies at St David's University College, Lampeter. He was educated at Oxford and Cambridge as well as Birmingham University, obtaining a degree in Theology and training for the ministry. Throughout these six years there was no discussion on the question of life after death, an omission which he decided to rectify.

After five years as a rector in Birmingham he went to Lampeter and launched an M.A. course on "Death and Immortality". He is now the most widely known thinker on life after death, having written "Christian Beliefs about Life after Death", "Immortality or Extinction?" and "Death and Immortality in the Religions of the World".

In Search of Heaven

"How I long for the lions!" wrote St Ignatius, travelling to his death in the Colosseum at Rome. For he delighted in the thought that as soon as the big cats had torn him to pieces he would find himself in heaven with Christ.

Such an attitude to death, let alone to the manner of his dying, seems utterly remote to us today. For almost all of us now, Christian and non-Christian alike, it is this life that absorbs all our interests, concerns and expectations. Think of our common expressions like, 'after all you've only got one life', or notice how often Church dignitaries are at pains to stress that 'Christianity is not concerned merely with life after death'. Yet, if one thinks about it, that is a very odd sentiment for any believer to express. After all, what could possibly be mere about living for ever! That such an expression is used implies that for many contemporary Christians life after death has become a purely formal belief, acknowledged in principle, but not taken into account in practice. Only in this light can we understand the words of a Churchwarden who said, 'after death I believe I shall enjoy everlasting bliss, but why discuss such a depressing subject now!'

One major reason for the decline in a positive future hope is a sense of unreality about the traditional language. Heaven seems too boring, and hell too dreadful, to be taken seriously. And what is really meant by talk of resurrection or immortality? Can we really look forward to the standing-up-again of the corpses, which is a literal translation of what the Communion creed actually says? I don't think so, and nor do any Church leaders, or they would have put this clause in modern English in the new service books, along with the rest of the creed. On the other hand, can one really believe that at the moment of death, some non-material part of us – the soul – will leave our bodies and go off on its own? And if it did would this be enough to count as survival?

Serious answers need to be given to questions like this, if

the future hope is to regain any real credibility. I happen to believe that answers are available, and that the Christian hope in immortality and resurrection can be spelt out in ways which do make sense, and which do not conflict in any absolute sense with other knowledge we have today about the nature of reality. But it must be acknowledged that in most Church quarters nowadays the hard questions are generally ducked by embarrassed Church spokesmen, and hence the case for heaven usually goes by default. This has profound consequences for faith. For without an eternal dimension, Christianity simply collapses into incoherence. This is not just my opinion: it was one of St Paul's central convictions that without a resurrection hope "we have nothing to preach, and you have nothing to believe".

Christianity burst upon the world explicitly as a religion of salvation, offering mankind for the first time a sense of utter and joyful certainty about a life to come: "an eternal weight of glory beyond all comparison" with our present earthly existence. All the first Christians thought of heaven as their true home, and came to think of themselves as "no more than strangers or passing travellers on earth". It was their absolute faith in the life beyond which enabled so many of the early Christians to embrace martyrdom with composure – and even with enthusiasm – and thereby to convert their persecutors. And in the mission field too it was the claim to know of an eternal life that was seen as Christianity's distinctive attraction. Certainly, according to the Venerable Bede it was the message of life after death which persuaded our Anglo-Saxon ancestors to embrace Christianity.

Throughout the Christian centuries, belief in a future life remained at the heart of all living faith. And this is not in the least surprising. After all, the essence of the Christian understanding of God is that he loves each one of us, and that within this life we can experience real fellowship and communion with God through prayer, worship and participation in life. Yet if we can truly enter a personal relationship with God which God values, and if each person as a unique individual really matters to the all-powerful and all-loving God, then God will not allow that individual and that relationship to be destroyed at death.

If death means extinction, this faith in God's love would be shown to be ultimately worthless. For nothing is more certain than that old age, disease and death await us all. And if God's power and love cannot extend into this realm, then he is not the Almighty Father of Christian conviction. In fact, St Paul summed up the position exactly when he wrote, "If it is for this life only that Christ has given us hope, we of all people are most to be pitied".

If we turn from belief in God to other Christian doctrines, we find exactly the same situation. None of them retains any real significance if divorced from faith in a life beyond. According to the creeds, the incarnation of God in Christ took place "For us men and for our salvation". If we have no ultimate salvation, it is hard to see what purpose the doctrine serves. Likewise with the belief in the resurrection of Jesus Christ: clearly it is possible to believe in the resurrection of Jesus as an event wholly unique to him and entailing no consequences for the rest of humanity. But in this case it is hard to see why it should be of any interest now, apart perhaps as a historical belief about the founder of Christianity. By contrast, the Christian tradition itself has seen the resurrection of Jesus as important precisely as a guarantee of a destiny in which we may expect to share. For St Paul, the whole point of Christ's resurrection was that it proved that death did not have final dominion. This was the message which the Church came into being to proclaim, which the New Testament was written to record, and which Christians throughout the ages have seen as the distinctive ground for their faith in the life of the world to come.

Similarly, if we look at the Christian sacraments, every one of them has a distinctly otherwordly theme. Thus at baptism a Christian is said to become an inheritor of the Kingdom of Heaven, and reference to God's everlasting Kingdom is made at the most solemn moments of confirmation, marriage, ordination, and absolution. In the Holy Communion Christians are given the bread of immortality in the Orthodox Liturgy, or the bread of eternal or everlasting life in Anglican and Roman formularies, and finally in the last rites the Christian receives the Viaticum to nourish his soul for the journey through death.

Hence it is not in the least surprising that with the collapse of any confident faith in a future life, Christianity in Europe has gone into a spiral of decline. Eighty years ago an eminent researcher in the psychology of religion, William James, found that for almost all believers of his day God primarily mattered as the provider of immortality. If God has ceased to matter to many Europeans, this may well reflect an intuitive judgement about the emptiness of Christian claims in a context where there is so little confidence about a future life.

But it is no accident that confidence in life after death has been eroded in our society. For many of the traditional descriptions of the future state are incredible to any one with the slightest acquaintance with modern knowledge, and contemporary attempts to restate the doctrine in more acceptable terms are not yet widely known. Christians used to believe that at the second coming of Jesus our corpses would be reassembled in their graves, the sea would give up its dead and the cannibal restore the flesh he had borrowed. We would then be restored to the state we were in before our final illness, or in some accounts, to what we were in the prime of life at around the age of thirty. Then we would all be judged by Christ and proceed either to heaven in the sky just above the earth, or to endless torture in a lake of fire below. And this is no caricature of Christian doctrine. Consider for example Tertullian's assertion that the reason Jesus had said "even the hairs of your head are all numbered" was that the numbering of each individual hair helped God to collect the various bits of us together again. Or think of St Augustine's long discussion in the "City of God" about how resurrected bodies will be able to stay up in the sky despite being heavier than air, or his description of Etna and Vesuvius as vent-holes of hell. Finally let us simply record the ultimate blasphemy perpetrated by Christian dogma in the twelfth century that one of the greatest joys of heaven would be to look down on the damned being tortured.

Obviously, no contemporary Christian would wish to defend the traditional scheme as it stands. The cosmological discoveries of the seventeenth century simply rule out the traditional identification of heaven with the sky, and the conscience of mankind, formed in part by a re-evaluation of

Jesus's essential teaching, has risen up against the appalling character of earlier teaching about hell. However, many Christians would argue that the resurrection of the body does witness to something of permanent importance. It cannot of course be taken literally. Modern biology teaches us that our bodies are not composed of distinctive particles which belong to us permanently, but rather that we are all made up of an ever recycling process of life. For example, 60% of our body-weight is water, and if we live in London the water we drink will have passed on average through five human intestines since it last fell from the clouds. Hence the material of which my body happens to be composed at the moment of death can in no sense be regarded as necessary to my continued identity at a final resurrection.

On the other hand, it does seem vital to our personhood that we should be embodied creatures capable of mutual recognition and action. Hence many Christian thinkers today, while rejecting belief in the future resuscitation of their corpses, do believe that in the life of the world to come our personality will be clothed in a new body for the continued expression of our selfhood. That is certainly the view of the Archbishop's Commission on Doctrine in the Church of England and it is very widely held among contemporary Christian scholars. It may also have been the very earliest Christian position. In Jesus's only recorded comment about the nature of life after death he described the literal view held by the Pharisees of his day as quite wrong, saying that in the next life men and women would be "like angels in heaven". St Paul believe that "flesh and blood cannot inherit the Kingdom of God" and that we will be given new "spiritual bodies". He clearly believed that in some sense we will continue after we have left our home in the body at death, but he thought that in the next life we will not simply be disembodied souls, for our inner nature will have a new body put on over it so that our mortal part may be absorbed into life immortal.

But is this a thinkable possibility? It certainly faces formidable objections. If we are talking of us getting new bodies we have to be prepared to face the question 'where is heaven?' Bodies require to be located, and there seems something very strange about the idea of planets elsewhere in our universe evolving with a similar biosphere to our own, and with all the ingredients necessary to sustain life just so that resurrected earthmen and women can drop in out of the blue and live there for ever and ever. However, at this point modern physics slightly eases the situation, because Einstein has shown that it is logically possible for there to be any number of different space-time systems in no relationship whatever to each other, provided that each is subject to different physical laws. Consequently we can speculate that the resurrection world (heaven) is in no spatial relationship whatsoever to our present universe, and that this quite other world would provide a wholly new kind of environment for our further development and advance. This would of course tie in with St Paul's view that heaven transcends anything we could visualise or expect: "things beyond our seeing, things beyond our hearing, things beyond our imagining, all prepared by God for those who love him." But it must be stressed that there is no evidence to support the existence of such a world, and our re-creation there would depend wholly on divine miracle. If on the basis of an overall Christian vision we believe in this, we are not actually in conflict with any other knowledge. Yet faith is certainly taking a bold leap when it jumps from a highly speculative possibility to a confident belief.

Many contemporary philosophers would not even concede this. They argue that it is precisely our present physical embodiment which makes us the people we are. If we are really to have wholly new bodies, for a radically different kind of existence, in what sense could we be the same persons? I believe that it is my thoughts, memories and self-awareness that makes me 'me', and though these may require require a physical substratum of some kind it would not effect my sense of self-identity if it turned out that they had been transcribed into a new and different body. I do not know whether the music I am listening to now comes from a magnetic tape, a plastic record, or a live broadcast, and similarly it would not effect my memories being my memories, if they were recorded on RNA in my present brain, as some believe they are now, or recorded on XYZ in a new

129

resurrection body. Besides, there is at least some evidence
that minds and brains are separable. And if this turns out to
be the case then the problem would not even arise. Either
way, it does seem plausible to claim that I could still be 'I'
even if clothed with a new and different body, provided only
that this new body was equally suitable as a vehicle for the
expression of my distinctive thoughts, feelings, and self-
awareness.

But this theory faces a third objection. This time it comes
from Christians, who ask how this understanding of resurrection can possibly be squared with the gospel picture of
Jesus's resurrection which appears to state unequivocally that
Jesus rose physically from his tomb, leaving it empty. Hence
to describe resurrection in terms of us getting new and
different bodies for a wholly different mode of existence cuts
the link with the historic interpretation of Easter which is
that Jesus rose from the dead in the same body, even though
that body was gloriously transformed.

There is no doubt that as far as it goes this objection is
valid. It is a plain matter of fact that for centuries a literal
understanding of Jesus's resurrection has been used as the
corner-stone for faith in a literal understanding of resurrection
for everyone else. Yet no appeal to this interpretation of the
resurrection of Jesus can alter the fact that belief in the re-
assemblage and re-vivifying of every human being who has
ever lived is impossible to square with our knowledge of the
place of man in an ever-recycling process of life. At the same
time, however, it has also become clear that the traditional
interpretation of Jesus's resurrection cannot be reconciled
with other strands in the New Testament evidence which
suggest that the earliest form of resurrection belief was
very different from the literalistic view which ultimately
triumphed.

Consider for example the view of many scholars that
St Paul knew nothing of the empty tomb tradition. Certainly
his denial that flesh and blood could ever inherit the
Kindgom of God seems hard to reconcile with any kind of
belief that Jesus's flesh and blood had already done so!
Likewise St Paul's remark that he would like to leave his
home in the body and go to live with the Lord seems to

presuppose that the Lord had left his earthly body as well. Moreover, the whole point of the sustained contrast that St Paul draws between earthly and heavenly bodies would be lost if he believed that there was any straightforward physical continuity between the two types of embodiment.

But St Paul certainly believed in the resurrection, and indeed saw it as the foundation stone of all his beliefs. So what did he believe about the resurrection? The most striking fact is that he placed the whole weight of his belief onto a conviction that Jesus had truly appeared to his disciples and he gives a long list of all these appearances, before adding "last of all he appeared also to me". Now the word Paul uses is *ophthe*, a word used to describe religious visions rather than physical sightings, and it is precisely as a heavenly vision that Paul thought of Christ's appearance to him. "God revealed his Son within me" is a literal translation of another of St Paul's accounts of his vision, which he took to be exactly the same kind of experience as that enjoyed by the first disciples. St Paul had no doubt of the reality of this vision. It transformed his whole life to see the risen Lord. Yet he was also sure that it was no resuscitated earthly body that he had seen, but rather a vision of the glory that lies ahead. For while a physical body had been buried, it was a spiritual body that had been raised.

The same understanding of Jesus's resurrection can be found in the first letter of Peter, where we read "in the body Jesus was put to death; in the spirit he was brought to life", and because this had happened to Jesus, Peter believed Christians are now born anew to a living hope and can expect of the dead that although in the body they received the sentence common to all men, they might in the spirit be alive with the life of God.

I suggest therefore that the earliest form of resurrection belief in the New Testament, and that which inspired and gave life to the first disciples, was a conviction that Jesus had triumphed over death and had communicated the fact of his aliveness to the minds of his disciples by a series of visionary experiences. The empty tomb tradition developed later because the wish of the disciples to stress the reality of what they had experienced led to the stories being given an increasingly physical character. Yet it is interesting how even the most physical of the gospel stories contain elements of the earlier tradition, as when Jesus is said to appear and disappear through locked doors, or when we are told that some of the disciples worshipped him, but others doubted.

In fact we know when the empty tomb story first began to circulate, for St Mark's gospel in its original form ends with a description of three women finding Jesus' tomb, and comments that the women said nothing about it to anyone because they were afraid. This tells us that the story was not part of the generally received traditions about Jesus before Mark's gospel came to be written. For it would be manifestly absurd for Mark to say that the women had said nothing about it to anyone, if the story of their finding the tomb empty had geen generally known. The comment in fact only makes sense if Mark was conscious that he was adding a new story to the tradition which had not been heard of before and which therefore he had to account for by the incredible notion that the women had for thirty years been silent about it.

(Repetition) I conclude therefore that the dynamic faith in a future life which launched the Christian Church into existence was based on a conviction that Jesus had triumphed over the crucifixion of his body and had revealed the fact of his living reality to the minds of his disciples by a series of real, but inwardly experienced, visions of himself. That in fact the resurrection of Jesus is the best attested and most influential instance of a deceased person appearing to the minds of some who had known him well during life, and that it is similar in kind to other cases which have been profoundly influential on the individuals who experienced them but which have not had the same public impact.

To some Churchmen it may seem almost blasphemous to suggest that Jesus's resurrection appearances were not unique, but belong to a class of phenomena well known to psychical research. Yet at the grass-roots of Christian experience this will not cause any concern at all. When working in ordinary parishes as a priest, I was constantly struck by how often the *de facto* ground for belief in life after death was confidence in an apparitional vision of a deceased loved one which had convinced the experiencer that all was well, and that death was not the end.

This kind of experience must not be confused with the deliberately sought-out kind practised in 'spiritualist' circles for which there is little to be said. But the spontaneous cases are in a different category and to those who have the experiences they are often convincing. Such cases, and indeed all purported evidence supportive of belief in a future life, cannot give any data about our ultimate destiny, but may, if valid, support belief in a mind-dependent world immediately following death.

According to the latest pronouncement of the present Pope: "The Church affirms that a spritual element survives and subsists after death, an element endowed with consciousness and will, so that the 'human self' subsists, though deprived for the present of its complement of the body." Similar teaching is to be found in Islamic thought in the concept of Barzakh and in Tibetan Buddhism in the notion of a Bardo-world. In fact all the great religions unite in teaching that immediately after death we will pass to a temporary mind-dependent world before resurrection in Islam, Christianity and Judaism, or reincarnation in Hinduism and Buddhism. And there is at least some evidence today which offers *prima facie* support for the existence of this state.

I have already mentioned the reported visionary appearances of the recently deceased, but much more telling are the direct accounts given by resuscitated people about the vivid experiences they claim to have enjoyed while hovering on the brink of death. Although the majority of the resuscitated remember nothing, those who do remember claim to have a very distinctive series of experiences which are reported with near unanimity from young and old, men and women, educated and illiterate, and from every national and religious grouping. When thousands of people from wholly different backgrounds testify to a common experience it does seem worth taking their reports seriously. One common factor is that at the moment of apparent death they found themselves out of their bodies looking down with interest on the resuscitation attempts. After recovery they accurately described what was going on when they were unconscious, and their perspective was from a point of view quite different from that of the body on the operating table. Dr R.A. Moody, who pioneered the current interest in this research, says, "physicians have reported to me that they just can't understand how their patients could have described the things they did about the resuscitation attempts, unless they really were hovering just below the ceiling". Following up this research, cardiologist Michael Sabom has tested in detail the reports of his patients, and has established that their statements are astonishingly correct, and cannot be explained on the basis of any familiarity with cardiac procedures, for study of a control group of cardiac patients who had not had the experience showed them not to have any real idea of what actually happens in such circumstances.

What is of crucial importance in all these cases is not the sensation of thinking that one is out-of-the-body, for a whole host of medical and psychological factors could easily account for this. But what such explanations cannot account for is the correct observations made. These seem to require the hypothesis that the persons concerned really did go out for their bodies. Yet if consciousness can, even for only a moment at the brink of death, think, observe and remember from a different perspective from that of the physical brain, then brain and mind must be separable, and the most weighty objection to even the possibility of immortal continuity has been removed. Those who have this experience are never in any doubt about the factuality of it, and, whatever their previous beliefs, they are from henceforth certain that there is life after death.

Three further features are also common to these accounts. Most claim to see deceased relatives and friends welcoming them into the world beyond, many claim to see a being of light which they usually identify with a figure in their own religious tradition, and some see a panoramic review of events of their past life. Clearly, these visions are mind-dependent since the relatives are seen as they were remembered in life, and the being of light is named in accordance with the percipient's own faith. Yet all who have such experiences are certain of their authenticity. In the nature of the case no one who has not had the experiences can really comment on their authenticity or otherwise, except perhaps in the case of little children. For children of four or five are not generally thought capable of understanding the implications of death, and at a time of psychological stress would be expected to hallucinate protective visions of their parents. In such cases the fact that only deceased relatives are seen might be thought significant, particularly when accurate descriptions are given of welcoming relatives who the dying child had never met in the brief span of its life.

There is therefore at least some support from the data of near-death experiences that after death we may enter a mind-dependent world. And it is interesting that if this is so, my suggestion that the appearances of Jesus to his disciples should be understood as some kind of telepathically communicated vision would cohere well with what communication in and from a mind-dependent world would actually be like.

However, all the major religions of the world unite in seeing a mind-dependent world as being in the long run an unsatisfactory mode of existence. As Aquinas put it, a disembodied soul exists in a deprived and unnatural state. Hence we may speculate that a mind-dependent world would be followed by resurrection to a new life in another space. Indeed, Professor John Hick has argued cogently that many lives in many worlds, with intervals for reflection in mind-dependent existences, would be the most suitable means for our personal development and spiritual progress towards God. Hick notes that this idea is a feature of much Eastern religious thought and although popular Hinduism talks of re-incarnation taking place on this planet, there are many references in both Hindu and Buddhist scriptures to future existences taking place in other worlds, and, given this modification, their theories correspond closely to what Hick suggests from within the Christian tradition. And if we note also Islamic discussions about the intermediate state of Barzakh we could argue that this speculation draws into a unified and coherent thesis ideas to be found in all the world's major religious traditions. And although this theory has been recently developed by John Hick on the basis of his global study of world religion, the thesis can also be seen in embryonic form in the works of one of the most eminent fourth-century theologians, St Gregory of Nyssa, who wrote, "moving from one new beginning to the next the soul makes its way towards the Transcendent".

But how likely is this as a future destiny for the flesh and blood creatures we know ourselves to be? In favour of it, I would claim that it is internally coherent, and logically possible. It does not directly contradict what we know from the natural sciences, though it is in conflict with many of the presuppositions of a naturalistic world-view. There are *some* apparently valid data which appear to support at least the first stage of this schema. And it is necessarily required if we suppose that humanity's relationship with God is a reality, and that we live in a purposive creation.

Against this vision, the data of modern science suggest that mankind's origin and destiny are inextricably bound up with the life-processes of this planet, and that mankind's religious aspirations are in the end a delusion.

In the final analysis, belief in a future life depends entirely upon understanding reality in the context of a divine being. From a secular perspective, life after death may be a nonsense. Yet for any overall religious vision to be intelligible, the search for heaven would seem an essential part of man's religious quest.

PETER MULLEN

Peter Mullen is Vicar of Tockwith and Bilston in North Yorkshire, where he looks after two rural churches and their congregations while writing regularly for the Guardian. He has also published several semi-fictionalised accounts of the weird and wonderful life of a country parson.

He is an outspoken critic of both dogmatic fundamentalists who, he claims, demand the suspension of all critical faculty, and those liberals who have reduced Christianity to a barely recognisable allegory. Instead he believes that with the insight of modern psychology we can understand the eternal spiritual truths which Christ reveals – truths which are the key to understanding the nature of mankind. His books include "Rural Rites" and "Being Saved".

The Feminine side of God and Man

When we think of God we inevitably reveal the structure of our own minds, for the doctrine of God is the theological reflection of the mind of humankind. Theology and psychology are nothing more than the inside and outside of the same thing – our humanness.

And when we think about the issue of feminism and the place of women we must begin with humanity's reflections on the nature of God. For the entire history of the Judeo-Christian civilisation continues to exert a powerful influence over all our notions of woman.

The Judeo–Christian civilization is rampantly masculine. The first stories told to our children are full of manly, warlike deeds: man the servant of God; man as God's prophet; man the great, the divinely inspired leader of the tribe or the nation. The archetypal heroes of our tradition are Abraham, Jacob, Moses and Joshua and their sons, the great kings David and Solomon; the prophets Amos, Hosea, Isaiah, Jeremiah and Ezekiel. The character of John the Baptist is the last word in macho in his coat of camel's hair and living on locusts and wild honey; not to mention Jesus himself, the new Joshua, the Messiah and Son of Man; and St Paul who thought that women should be quiet in church.

All these men worshipped the one God, the Lord, the God of armies who was known for his wrath, for his warlike deeds on behalf of his people, for his leading the fierce tribes of Israel with a mighty hand and an outstretched arm. This is the God known to English readers of the bible as the Lord. His name in the ancient languages always connotes masculine power: he is God Almighty, God of the Mountains, God whose spirit lurks in the desert places where it whips up the sands into a fury. This God is in storm and tempest, in clouds and earthquakes; he pours fire and brimstone down on the sinful cities of the plain. In the gospel of St Matthew it is this same God who sits on his throne in judgement, separating the sheep from the goats, having the power to cast erring souls into the nethermost hell.

Genesis says that God made man in his own image. From the theological point of view, that is absolutely correct, orthodox. But from the psychological viewpoint it is man who makes God in man's own image. This is necessarily so, since all perceptions and conceptions, all doctrines and image-making are expressed by means of language: and language is a human creation. So God who inhabits the highest heaven is thought of in terms which owe their origin to the psychological make-up and political organisation of terrestial man. In the patriarchal world of the Old Testament, women are regarded as inferior to men. When they do get a chance to move to the centre of the stage, they are often shown as contributing to man's downfall: so it is Eve who, seduced by the serpent, issues the fatal temptation to Adam; and it is Sarah, Abraham's wife, who gets her husband into trouble by laughing at the angel of the Lord.

The Ten Commandments prohibit all forms of idolatry, but the Hebrew prophets particularly condemned those who worshipped the fertility goddesses of the Canaanite plain. God was one. God was to be obeyed. And God was male, a man of war. But this onesidedness, this extreme obsession with masculinity, could not be maintained for ever, despite the political and sociological forces operating in its favour. For a true understanding of human psychology shows that even the manliest man has his feminine side and that women share many of the male qualities. This understanding has been demonstrated in our own century by C.G. Jung and is supported by information gathered from genetic research. The androgynous nature of mankind has been attested throughout history, and it is a profound and persistent theme in most of civilization's great stories and myths.

Even the Old Testament cannot perpetually depict God as wholly masculine, divorced from all femininity. In Proverbs, Ecclesiastes and the Book of Wisdom the Lord God has a consort whose name is Wisdom. The word used is the Greek 'Sophia', a feminine noun. Man is urged in these books to seek wisdom as if involved in an act of courtship: from a psychological perspective this is the signal for man to pay attention to his intuitive, feminine qualities and so harmonise his nature by integrating its different aspects. In the book of the prophet Hosea, God himself begins to exhibit a quality of tenderness: he is portrayed as the loving husband of an unfaithful wife – Israel. The redemption of the erring, harlot nation Israel in Hosea's book comes about through a union of masculine and feminine aspects. And, according to Jung, this is an image of what must happen in the soul or psyche of every man (and every woman too) if he is to become whole, integrated, balanced. Or, as the older theological language puts it, redeemed and saved.

Of course, man is stubborn, and he often resists the way to his own integration. He denies his feminine side. We see this in many forms throughout history. It is there in St Paul's mysogynism and in St Augustine's fear of women which he translated into a furious and fanatical insistence on the overriding merits of virginity. It is there, too, in the witch-hunts of the Middle Ages and in the Church's obsession with sexual sins – even when orthodoxy itself insists that the sins of the flesh are not as serious or as destructive as the sins of the spirit, such as pride which, in biblical mythology, was at the source of Satan's original disobedience. But even in our own supposedly liberal age, it is still sexual offences which attract the strongest disapproval: we do not hear of ladies having been dismissed from the Mothers' Union on account of excessive pride! But let a churchgoer be a discovered adulterer and see how quickly and how fiercely denunciation and ostracism ensue.

The life and work of Jesus did much to restore the balance between masculine and feminine aspects. Women were little better than slaves in the man's world of first-century Palestine. But Jesus went out of his way to associate with them. Not all of these women were entirely respectable: it is widely believed, for example, that Mary Magdalene either was or had been a prostitute. In St John's gospel, Jesus refuses to condemn the woman taken in adultery – "in the very act". It is women who stand by the cross when the manly disciples have fled to save their own skins. Women anoint his body for the burial. And women are the first witnesses to the resurrection: "The first day of the week cometh Mary Magdalene early, when it was yet dark, unto the sepulchre."

Christian teaching about the incarnation and the virgin birth represents a great advance on old masculine, Jewish mentality. For here the great masculine God, the high and mighty Lord of Lords, the only ruler of princes, depends for his greatest revelation of himself upon the willing cooperation of a young Jewish girl. We wonder how St Paul squared his anti-feminism with the tradition of divine partnership with woman as revealed by the doctrine of the virgin birth. Perhaps we wonder also, in an age when Bishops are fond of airing their doubts about the virgin birth, whether their denials do not tell us more about themselves and their own unconscious psychological rejection of femininity in religion than about the alleged facts concerning Our Lady.

In the history of the Church and of Christian spirituality, there have been many women who were not content to remain passive but who exercised powers of spiritual insight and leadership, founding religious orders and institutions, even preaching the word of God and, in the archetypal character of Joan of Arc, leading armies. Mother Julian of Norwich, in her visions out of which she compiled "Revelations of Divine Love", claimed that God is our mother as well as our father. And the frequently androgynous character of angels in Christian art and iconography shows a desire to represent spiritual reality as composed of both masculine and feminine aspects. That is a theological representation. Its psychological correlative is to be found in the very down to earth truth that, in his inner life no less than in his outward behaviour, man requires woman for his completion. And she requires him.

Jung divides man's soul or psyche into two parts: conscious and unconscious. Man's consciousness is masculine. His unconscious is feminine. Jung calls the unconscious feminine aspect the anima. This is a very powerful image, literally pregnant with meaning. For it is the anima – literally that which gives life, enlivens – which urges man on to deeds of bravery and to the creative expression of his true self. The best way to envisage the work of the anima is to move away from the abstract terminology of analytical psychology and to see the actual personification of the feminine principle in the great and abiding works of Western literature and culture. Those stories of gods and goddesses are not just fairytales. They are not so trivially dismissed. For the tales we tell reveal what manner of persons we are.

In the growth and integration of our personalities, conscious and unconscious aspects must develop together in a mutually creative relationship. And, just as the conscious, observable boy-man must progress from childishness, in experience and maturity to the full stature of manhood, so his unconscious aspect must develop too. We may catalogue man's development in stages like Shakespeare's seven ages of man: baby, child, youth, soldier, lover, accomplished adult and wise old man. The unconscious aspect, the anima, or woman-within, goes through a similar process of maturing and transformation from weakness to perfection. This process can be fascinatingly observed in the great myths and poems of our civilization.

Her history parallels the development of the objective woman. First she is seen in all those stories of childhood innocence. This is the anima pre-puberty when, though she may evoke images of a childlike, paradisal existence, she is yet unawakened, impotent, unamoured. Images are of Eliot's "children in the apple tree" – boy and girl (conscious and unconscious forces) existing together in a paradisal, timeless world which does not yet know the ecstasy and the burden of sexual union. Usually in the paradisal myths, the heavenly children do not work. Nothing is achieved. All is simply given. Work and progress begins with the traumatic events of arousal and intercourse. This symbolises the conscious and unconscious forces first becoming aware of each other and realising that mutual co-operation, though painful, is absolutely necessary. As Sisson wrote, this sexual union is not just as "the rutting stage knows; it is to take Eve's apple and lose the paradisal look."

This is the transition from the pre-sexual world of childhood when male and female personalities co-operate – but without knowing their true adult nature and purpose – to the adult world of sexual initiation. The first stirrings of sexual arousal tell us who we are and what our purpose is.

The symbolism is explicit in the Genesis story: we eat of the tree of knowledge. And in the biblical Hebrew, the word for knowledge is the same as that for the sex act. This is also the stage when the anima becomes temptress. Eve tempts Adam and he succumbs. But this is not a story found only in the Hebrew bible. It is there too in Babylonian and other Near-Eastern myths. It is found in Greek culture in the story of the exotic Sirens, the temptresses who would lure Ulysses and all sailors onto the rocks. It is there in the romantic legends about wood-nymphs and the Lorelei who charm men to distraction.

Some feminists object to this description of the anima because they see it as necessarily showing women in a poor light, putting all the blame on her for men's ills. In fact, their apprehension is quite needless. Man must fall in order to rise, that is to become a whole, integrated human being. That is the message of all those myths about Sirens and Temptresses. And the balance is ultimately redressed for, as we shall see, woman who is responsible for man's downfall is also the cause of his final redemption – a religious way of talking about his full maturity and integration of the personality.

The image of the Temptress did not fade with the passing of ancient or classical culture. She is there in Hollywood, in the femme fatale, in every Siren and Temptress from 'the It-Girl' to Marilyn Manroe and the sexy Madonna (a very revealing title, in the context of the psychological-religious understanding of man's sexual and personal development!) The archetype of the Temptress in modern and popular culture can be well seen in works such as Alban Berg's opera "Lulu", in Joseph von Sternberg's famous film "The Blue Angel" and in Monroe's exasperating, fascinating role in "Seven Year Itch". There are more common examples in the pouting, posturing femmes fatales in "Dallas" and "Dynasty" as well as in the models who smile at men from the various page threes of daily tabloids. She is *She*: 'She who must be obeyed': Desire(e).

If a man is to achieve proper maturity, he must learn to leave behind the stage of sexual enchantment symbolised and represented by the Temptress, the Siren and the Lorelei. He must learn a proper perspective, a sense of adjustment to the world's realities. That is, he must acquire wisdom; wisdom, as we have seen, is personified in our cultural tradition as Sophia, the consort of God. Man is made, says scripture, in the image of God. So man, developing according to the divine pattern, must find that balance in the mature relationship between his consciousness and his anima that is expressed in the theological picture of the Lord with his consort Sophia. In external, objective terms, the anima–as–Sophia stage is personified in a man's relationship with his wife, which, it is to be hoped, still retains a sexual element but which puts sex into the context of a practical commitment to daily tasks, to working out a life together not so much in the heat and rush of the early sexual experiences, but in the shared life of mutual responsibility.

From Girl-Child to Temptress and Sophia, the anima as a man's unconscious develops in a positive, creative way. The man learns about his inwardness, and his inwardness gives him power – literally inspires, animates him – so that he can continue to make progress towards full integration of the personality: to what in the older religious language was called salvation and redemption. The anima–as–Sophia stage may also be seen as the stage of the wife or companion. And the archetypal expression of the couple is not, at this stage, the erotic coupling of Faust and Gretchen, Tristan and Isolde or Romeo and Juliet: it is the mature stage of the wifely companion – what the bible calls 'helpmeet' – personified by such as Dante and Beatrice on their worldly-spiritual pilgrimage.

This is the period of marriage. Theologically, it can be represented as marriage between the Lord and his people Israel, as in Hosea; sociologically, it corresponds to the institution of marriage as prescribed by society; psychologically, it is the partnership and growing union between the conscious and unconscious aspects in the personality. We are talking about the very structure of the human personality – an older age would have used the word 'soul' which is, in any case, the word for the Latin 'anima' – so we should not expect images and representations of this universal condition to be restricted to orthodox theology and religious or secular high art. We are talking about every man's story. So, as in the

144

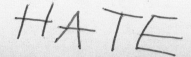

examples from popular literature and films of the Temptress or femme fatale, we see in those same sources popular personifications of the comparison. There are, for instance, the exciting stories of the opening up of the West in the U.S.A.: the waggon-trains were driven by the heroes who were always supported by their wives, 'the womenfolk'. It is the image of the pilgrimage. When the couple as partners are attacked by hostile forces, they drive their waggons into a ring. The ring or circle, like the wedding ring, is the symbol of perfection, completion.

The final personification of the anima is as Virtue itself. Archetypally, this is seen clearest in our Judeo-Christian tradition in the person of the Blessed Virgin Mary. Because of her obedience, her perfect virtue, she becomes, according to traditional doctrine, the Mother of God, God-bearer.

Now at last the circle is complete. Scripture says, "As in Adam all men die, so in Christ shall all be made alive." The feminine counterparts in this masculine economy are, of course, Eve and Mary. As man was seduced by woman, so he is also saved by her. None of this is meant to cast a slur on particular women, and the feminist antagonism to anima-psychology is, in my opinion, misplaced. I have only described psychological processes as they actually occur and as they are pictured in the art and literature of our culture and civilization. Those myths and legends are not trivial. They tell the truth. They are our story. The circle is completed. Man who falls because of Eve is raised because of Mary. A new man is born – the Christchild – and the process is begun all over again in the iconography of religious symbolism and in the life of every man. The anima is both good and bad, creative and destructive, just as the conscious mind is also good and bad, capable of issuing both blessings and curses.

Religious stories as found in the bible are the basic raw material by which a civilization understands itself. It was well said that every culture writes its poetic epics at the beginning of its course. All that follows is an attempt to tell the old story in new words. And the many stories that are told serve to personify in exciting and pictorial style the endlessly repeated programme of man's inner development, his moral and spiritual pilgrimage. How could things be otherwise? A mystery which does not reveal some truth about us is always rejected as uninteresting. We find certain stories eternally fascinating, for they put into images the most profound spiritual-psychological truths about what it is to be a human being. And our various re-tellings of primitive myth and saga are not mere repetition: each new tale is itself, told in the cultural garb, in the thought-forms and language of a particular historical time and place. I will give some examples from so-called 'high' and 'popular' art of different ages. We should not despise the popular versions, for they are the means by which the many participate in the understanding which high art mediates to the few.

The Romantic Age's reworking of the bible's pictorialisation of man's craving for wholeness, integration of the personality and salvation is to be found in Goethe's Faust. Here is the man, the hero, Everyman who encounters his anima in all her various guises. He meets Gretchen as a child, loves her as a Siren and even kills her. But at the end of his life she appears as an angel from heaven to redeem him. She is virtue personified: Grace. The story is wonderfully and evocatively told. And it is gloriously translated into musical terms in the Symphony Number Eight by Gustav Mahler. This ends with the appearance of the heavenly choir who, in Goethe's words, give musical expression to the story of man's salvation:

"All things transitory
Are as symbols sent;
Earth's insufficiency
Here finds fulfilment;
Here the ineffable
Wins life through love
The Endless Woman-Soul [i.e. the anima]
Leads us above."

It should be said that the anima is one. She has many guises, but she herself is a unity. This means that in all the later stages of her development she yet contains the earlier ones. This is also the important difference between caricature and real character. The mature woman occasionally reveals the child or the Temptress in her. This is the undeniable principle of continuity in the development of human personality which raises human beings above the level of mere mechanism, mere organism – so beloved of the inhuman behavioural sciences – and makes life really lively (erotic) and immediate, tangible, not ghostly or abstract. Shakespeare's phrase "too solid/sullied flesh" comes to mind.

All those fairytales about the Prince who hacks his way through the dense wood to find his Princess (his anima, his soulmate) tell the same story of each man's pilgrimage of self-discovery through the integration of his female aspects. And the story repeats itself in suitable technological garb in our own age in films such as Star Wars and even in the popular television series Dr Who. This is not fanciful. We must learn not to be surprised when popular art gives expression to the story of Everyman. Indeed, what else should we expect any human storytelling to do except tell us something about the storytellers – ourselves?

The character Dr Who is a modern technological variant on the ancient gnostic Redeemer figure who comes from the supernatural world, armed with his secret knowledge and magic potions and powers to banish evil and right the terrestial world of all wrongs. This figure was very popular in Middle-Eastern theology and mythology in the first few centuries AD. Now, in the sci-fi mode, Dr Who does just the same in our era. He is a Lord of Time or Time-Lord who comes from a world that is beyond time. He too brings his superior knowledge, his TARDIS or machine which can transcend time and his many other magical gadgets. Like the gnostic Redeemer, he finds himself up against evil powers and principalities, spiritual wickedness in high places. Dr Who, over twenty-one years of programmes, has always had a female assistant. It is marvellously supportive of the idea of the universality of the anima figure that, in a popular series like this one, the assistant should develop and change precisely according to the sequence of the anima's development in classic spirituality, mythology and human personality. At first she was a little child, Sarah. Then she became the savage Temptress, Leela. The next incarnation was into the virtuous companion, Romana. And the final stage was the elevation of Romana to the rank of Time-Lady, so that she became the equal of the Doctor, the contemporary incarnation of the gnostic Redeemer. Since this pattern of the anima's development is a universal phenomenon, we should not be in the least surprised to find it occurring wherever stories are told. It is not usually a conscious manipulation of symbolism by the writer but an eruption into consciousness of undeniable unconscious contents.

Jung has much to say about the most popular of all personifications of divine femininity: the doctrine of the assumption of the Blessed Virgin into heaven. This was long believed by the mass of ordinary folk, as accounts in popular literature have shown for hundreds of years. And the Feast of the Assumption has been in the Church's calendar since the Middle Ages. What is new is the proclamation in November 1950 of the assumption as an infallible dogma and article of faith by the Pope. To Protestants and Rationalists this was a retrograde step, offending against the refined liberal-scientific prejudices of the age. But, as Jung said, the Pope was responding in the only way he could to an enormous popular demand for femininity to take its place in heaven and to become part of what is divine. The centuries of emphasis on the masculine God represented a disturbance in the balance between masculine and feminine which is the structure of the human psyche. The dogma of the assumption restores the balance. This has a profound practical effect for, in this final phase of the Christian aeon when man lives under the threat of a universal destruction of his own making, the emergence of the feminine, tender, merciful archetype may turn out to be one of our most hopeful signs: a sign of man's inner integration, of his learning to harmonise together the different aspects of his personality. And the image of the Virgin enthroned may become the most positively prophetic symbol of our time.

Finally, there is the need to show how all these eternal and pictorial images of the anima actually reflect themselves in the everyday life of the ordinary embodied man as he makes the journey through life from childhood to old age. It is time to look at the practical psychological events which are in every man the day by day working out of all this symbolism in common experience. What follows is a sort of brief psychological biography.

From an early age men and boys are likely to reject the feminine side of their nature. We see examples in the school playground: the odium attracted by any boy who goes in for playing with dolls or for following some of life's gentler callings such as art, music and poetry. He will be called 'pansy', or worse. And then throughout life there is a widespread tendency to despise homosexuals: the derogatory jargon used to describe them and the cruel jokes often made at their expense is as much evidence as we need. But what is hatred of homosexuals except a projected fear of the reality of our own femininity?

In our youth it is good, if rather painful at times, to have many love-affairs – that is to encounter and integrate the anima-archetype of the Temptress or Enchantress. She is a part of man's personality, the woman within; and, if she is not met and integrated at the time of our youth, she will only emerge neurotically later on in the well-known and sorry figure of the middle-aged man in constant pursuit of young mistresses. He is having to catch up on a phase that was missed earlier in his life. The young mistresses may be real enough in the flesh and blood, but the function they perform is as girls of his dreams. That unhappy, unbalanced forty-five-year-old has at last caught sight of his anima in her most lurid and sexually potent guise. The anima is unconscious. We fall into unconsciousness. The other expression is of 'falling in love'. Language always tells a story. And not just of forty-year-olds. Jung writes, "when a respectable septuagenarian runs off with a seventeen-year-old from the chorus line, we know that the gods have claimed another victim."

The anima represents the emotional, feeling, intuitive aspects of a man's personality. So the man who has not integrated his anima is likely to be over-controlled, insisting on the utter sovereignty of logic and the need for a rational explanation for everything. He may be over-intellectual, calculating, mean. He is not likely to have much patience with his flighty teenage daughters: their excessive feminine behaviour will be only a threat to his exquisitely guarded masculinity. He has so much to deny in himself, so much to shut out and disown. Hope may come to him through an understanding wife who will personify her husband's anima. And if he can form a constructive, self-giving relationship with his wife, 'that may be the way towards his own integration. Or, risking moral censure, he may find a mistress – someone near his own age who will be his soulmate and companion, the one in whom he can come to see his own inwardness reflected.

The man who has integrated consciousness with the unconscious anima will be more relaxed, gentler, more secure without having to flex his macho muscles all the while. He will have that sense of balance and perspective that finds its best and most human expression in a sense of humour. It has been said that a sense of humour is a sense of perspective dancing. Integration of consciousness and Anima is true balance, true perspective: so humour, the ability to laugh at oneself, is the mark of the mature and integrated man.

Similarly, the anima or unconscious aspect, like sleep, is closely associated with death. The integrated man who has his masculine and feminine aspects in balance will not fear death. His anima, his soul, is not destroyed by death – which was the old religious way of expressing that eternal truth.

Not only the Christian Church, then, but every man, has everything to gain by the sincere attempt to integrate masculine and feminine aspects. To do less is to fall into spiritual and psychological imbalance which always has had consequences for institutions and individuals alike. More open and honest reflection is needed. A willingness to look inward at ourselves and, when we do not always like what we see, still steadfastly to refuse simply to project our dislikes on to others, be they women priests, homosexuals or folk we are quick to accuse of sexual impropriety.

As even the rumbustious God of the Old Testament at last discovered, the choice is to remain in the cold, arid desert or to find the true consort, Sophia, the tender intuitive wisdom of maturity and integration, the soulmate, the anima and the woman-within.

MYRTLE LANGLEY

Myrtle Langley is the diocesan missioner on David Sheppard's staff in Liverpool and an honorary lecturer in theology at Manchester University. She was born in Tipperary in the Irish Republic and trained to be a teacher in Dublin. In 1966 she went to East Africa as a missionary and worked in Kenya, developing religious studies. She came to acquire a great respect for the religious traditions of the African people and returned to England to lecture on missionary life.

A great believer in the ordination of women, she has written a semi-autobiographical account of the relationship between women and the Church.

Living with Other Faiths

In 1855 an Amerindian chief wrote to the president of the United States of America: "One thing we know, that the white man may one day discover, our God is the same God. You may think that you own him as you wish to own our land, but you cannot." Yet, over a hundred years later, on 30 September 1966, I set sail for East Africa as a Christian missionary. I went with a conviction in my heart and a message on my lips: that Africa's peoples needed to know the God and Father of my Lord and Saviour Jesus Christ. I embarked on the last passenger voyage of the Kenya Castle. And with hindsight I have often thought how symbolic this was of the end of colonialism and the demise of the life-long career missionary, of which I was one of the last European examples.

I

I set out for Africa with a grounding in the arts and theology but with little knowledge or understanding of the continent, its peoples or its religions. I had undergone a classic evangelical conversion in my teens, a conversion to God and away from the world, making me somewhat pietistic and other-worldly. My theology or attitude towards other faiths and religions was *exclusivist*: I may not have considered the beliefs of non-Christians a demonic delusion but neither did I consider them to be sufficient for salvation. They were at the very least idolatrous and at their very best mere religions, as against true faith – the inadequate product of human imagination rather than the fruit of divine revelation.

An enquiring mind, a wealth and depth of new personal experience and a number of telling encounters with people of other faiths came to my rescue. As a result, my discipleship of Jesus changed from being in the nature of a fixed focus on his and my relationship with God to zooming in and out on the

152

implications of Christian faith for life in the world; I began to think in terms of a second conversion – back to the world. And my attitude towards other religions underwent a process of re-orientation; I began to take up an *inclusivist* position – according adherents of other faiths some knowledge of truth and of God even if they were not complete apart from fulfilment in Jesus Christ. In this process of re-orientation I vividly recall three encounters which were to broaden my horizons and enrich my perceptions. They were with peoples of traditional Africa.

I was taking a stroll with a friend through the fields of Nandi country in the highlands of western Kenya. The late afternoon sun was warm, the air crisp and at times acrid with smoke wafting its way upwards through the thatched roofs of small homesteads dotted in clusters across the wide open marshes and grasslands. I was lecturing at the nearby teachers' college and quite frequently took a walk when afternoon classes had finished. This particular afternoon, however, we were stopped and greeted by an old woman. "Is it well?" she enquired. Fortunately, my friend was fluent in the local dialect, so we responded. "Is it well, old woman?" "Are you well?" she continued. "Yes," we replied. Whereupon she proceeded in the usual Nandi manner to enquire after husband, children and livestock. Perplexity and bewilderment, however, followed the disclosure that neither of us had a husband, either in Kenya or overseas (as she had suggested). Nevertheless, she went on, undaunted, to enquire after the children. (Imagine our amazement and amusement, very much like 'Victorian hands up in horror'!) No children. This was indeed impossible, unbelievable!

We parted on the understanding that she would make appropriate and discreet arrangements for the begetting of children, husband or not! Only later did I realise the full implications of her kind-hearted promise – for she was offering to arrange a precious 'woman marriage' for an unknown foreigner: 'woman marriage' being a process whereby a childless older woman is married to a younger woman who engages the services of a visiting genitor who provides the younger woman with a child whom the two women can then enjoy rearing together.

I was visiting an old man, a confirmed traditionalist and believer in the Nandi God, *Asis*. And I grew incredulous as he related with great sincerity how he had given up his beer-drinking. Beer-drinking had ritual significance for him and Nandi of the past, he averred, and lamented how the young boys and girls abused its significance by buying beer in bottles and cans from the shops. Such practice broke every rule of the gerontocracy sanctioned by *Asis*! Here was conviction of a puritanical kind such as I might have met among Northern Ireland Protestants or Scottish Calvinists – my theological forebears!

I was researching the history of Christian missions in Nandi when I heard one of the first Christian converts relate a memorable story. As a young boy he had been present when some of the early missionaries began to preach in the countryside. They were nicknamed by the people *kipsomasis*, literally 'those who keep begging God'. The Nandi knew well that at sunrise and before going on hunting and raiding expeditions, they prayed to *Asis* to 'bless the warriors, the children and the cattle'. They did not need to keep begging God in prayer, for they knew that he both heard their prayers and answered them. Was he not the beneficent creator, sustainer of life and arbiter of justice? Symbolized by the sun, did he not bestow light, rain and fertility? And had not the Nandi something to teach Christians about prayer?

I was not to know then that a new and exciting journey was just beginning: what was to become for me a voyage of theological discovery and a pilgrimage on which I would encounter a variety of people belonging to different races, cultures and faiths.

II

From Nandi I moved to Nairobi, a cosmopolitan city. There I found myself involved willy-nilly in a multicultural, multi-racial and multifaith society and teaching religious education to Hindus, Buddhists, Jains, Muslims and Baha'is as well as Christians. And so the question of pluralism had to be faced. Was it arrogant or even adequate in the context of this mixed society to believe that every other faith must find its fulfilment and centre in Jesus Christ? Perhaps we needed a Copernican revolution, placing God and not Jesus at the centre of the universe of faiths. I have not yet disembarked from the voyage and I am still engaged in the pilgrimage. Nevertheless, I continue to place Jesus Christ at the centre, considering the revelation of God in Christ as *unique* although not exclusive, while reminding myself constantly of certain stories about Jesus which we read in the gospels.

There are many ways in which Jesus in his time stands out as a person apart. The evangelist Luke, author of the third gospel, specifically depicts Jesus as 'the Man for outsiders': among whom he counts Gentiles (foreigners), Samaritans (people of mixed race and religion), tax-collectors (collaborators and rascals) and women (second-class citizens). The evangelist Matthew may insist for all his worth that Jesus's mission was first to Israel, but at the end of the day he does so only in order to strengthen his case for extending the offer of salvation to the nations in the aftermath of Jewish infidelity and rebelliousness.

Jesus spent most of his ministry in 'Galilee of the Gentiles' – an area with a large population of peoples of mixed race and mixed religion, with temples in addition to synagogues and miracle-workers as well as elders. The common language was neither Hebrew nor Aramaic but Hellenistic Greek and there was an obvious commingling of peoples along the borders. The Gospels tell us several stories about how Jesus related to some of these peoples, especially Samaritans and Gentiles within and without the borders.

In Luke we read of the Roman officer who approached Jesus, either directly or indirectly through friends, to ask for healing for his servant. The man was probably a Syrian Gentile in the army of Herod Antipas. But he obviously had enough respect for Judaism to have built a synagogue and to request help from a Jew. He also knew enough to be aware that a Jew might shrink from entering the house of a Gentile. The main interest of the story is to stress this Gentile officer's belief that Jesus had authority and power over sickness and disease such as he himself had over his soldiers. Such authority would even allow a word of command to be effective from a distance. And in response to such faith Jesus replied, "I tell you, not even in Israel have I found such faith." I am very much drawn to Jesus's recognition of faith as the key to this story.

One Christian commentator remarks that such faith revealed that the officer had been truly healed by God before his servant was cured of sickness by Jesus. Another illuminates the whole subject, commenting, "Jesus's surprise shows that faith is not simply assent to a particular doctrine – although it can include that – but, if genuine, faith will always express itself in vital forms. As a result, Jesus can say that he has never found such faith in 'anyone in Israel'."

Matthew states that the Kingdom of heaven is promised to all with such faith. Belief, of course, was already widespread in Israel since the time of Isaiah but there was no vision of a community comprising Gentiles and Jews. In Jesus we do find this startlingly new vision.

Each of the three Synoptic evangelists, Matthew, Mark and Luke, reports how on the death of Jesus it was a Roman officer who exclaimed at his innocence. Both Matthew and Mark report that he said, "Truly this (man) was the Son of God!" while Luke simply records the assertion, "Certainly this man was innocent!" The significance lies in the plain fact of a Gentile perceiving Jesus's innocence (or who he was) – a perception of faith – being set in stark contrast to the mockery of the people standing by. In addition one commentator makes the point that when Luke uses the phrase "praised God" or "glorified God" he means to indicate a response to a revelation of divine power and mercy. And it was a Roman officer rather than one of God's chosen people who "praised God" for the way Jesus died.

Both Matthew and Mark record Jesus's venturing outside Galilee into the district of Tyre and Sidon – Gentile territory. While there, a Greek woman, a Syrophoenician by birth, followed him into a house and begged him to help her daughter who was "possessed by a demon". The reply made by Jesus is notorious and much-debated: "Let the children first be fed, for it is not right to take the children's bread and throw it to the dogs." Did Jesus mean to use "dogs" in the sense of a Jewish pejorative term for Gentiles? Most scholars think not, because the Greek word is in the diminutive and means 'little dogs' or 'household pets'. The woman replied undaunted, with great persistence and not a little wit, "Yes, Lord; yet even the dogs under the table eat the children's crumbs." And she was rewarded for her 'faith': "For this saying you may go your way; the demon has left your daughter" (according to Mark) or "O woman, great is your faith! Be it done for you as you desire" (according to Matthew). Once again I note Jesus's awareness and appreciation of a Gentile's faith but also that neither on this nor any other such occasion is conversion recorded. And once again a commentator adds illuminatingly: "In the immediate context the faith of the Gentile woman, who is free from the law, stands out against the background of Jewish legalism, the absurdity of which is not recognized even by the disciples . . . the story must have been directed from the very beginning to the problem of the relation of the Gentiles to the Jews. Here . . . it is the faith of the Gentile which finds access to Jesus. In this experience the boundaries of Israel have been transcended, a feat which Jesus accomplished even though he seldom left the land of the Jews, encountered Gentiles only in exceptional cases, and did not launch any mission to them. If the decisive thing is no longer faithfulness to the law, but the attitude of faith to which Jesus is calling and which is presented here by way of an example, then the Gospel actually is offered to all nations."

Three incidents relating to Jesus and the Samaritans provide me with inspiration. The Samaritans were descended from a people who had compromised their Jewish race and religion and therefore there was little love lost between Jews and Samaritans; in fact, Samaritans were despised by Jews.

It is exhilarating to be able to observe that the pointers towards Jesus's recognition of faith in Gentiles and Samaritans which we are detecting throw some fresh light on one of the more difficult texts in the gospels. Such is the case with the healing of ten lepers recorded by Luke. Jesus healed ten lepers, telling them to go and demonstrate their healing to the priests. This they did but only one returned to give praise to God – a Samaritan – so that Jesus exclaimed, "Were not ten cleansed? Where are the nine? Was no-one found to return and give praise to God except this foreigner?" Then, turning to the Samaritan, he said, "Rise and go your way; your faith has made you well." The commentators are puzzled because the nine were also healed. Why should the tenth need to be 'healed' or 'saved' again? I believe that Jesus was in the latter instance alluding not to a request for healing but to that faith which praises God in response to the revelation of divine power and mercy.

In a similar frame of mind Jesus told the enquiring lawyer his famous parable or story of the good Samaritan – the traveller who stopped to help the man who had fallen among thieves. Jesus deliberately shocked the lawyer by forcing him to consider the possibility that a semi-pagan foreigner might know more about the love of God than a devout Jew blinded by preoccupation with pettifogging rules. Jews demanded love of God and love of neighbour. The love of God could be shown through following the whole Law with its 613 commandments. But the term 'neighbour' was one of limited liability and much time and energy were expended in debating what classes of people might be excluded. In his parable Jesus turned the tables and instead of answering the lawyer's question "Who is my neighbour?", asked "To whom should I be neighbour?" and replied "To anyone who is in need of my love." The exemplar of neighbourliness in the story is the outsider, the 'hated' Samaritan. I often compare the impact of the story on its time with the effect on neo-fascists today of the story of a turbaned Sikh calling an ambulance to a member of the National Front mugged on the streets of London!

And finally there is the incident recorded by John of Jesus at a well in Samaria asking drink of a woman who was a Samaritan and a sinner. On this occasion Jesus is reported as not only saying that "salvation is of the Jews" but that "the hour is coming, and now is, when the true worshippers will worship the Father in spirit and truth". Neither in Jerusalem nor on Mount Gerizim will he be worshipped, but in spirit and truth. The cultus is rejected, the particularities of both Jews and Samaritans queried. Significantly it was this person, three times an outsider – being at the same time a woman, a Samaritan and a sinner – who testified to Jesus as "the Saviour of the world".

And yet, irony of ironies, even as Jesus broke down barriers between Jew and Gentile, Christians of a later age re-erected them and perpetrated the crimes of anti-Semitism, often in the name of Christian particularity.

For me then, nurtured in the Christian community of faith, assenting to the authority of the Scriptures as they bear witness of Jesus Christ, the incarnate and living word of God, and seeking to follow in the footsteps of Jesus, living with other faiths implies an openness of approach. It implies a readiness to engage in genuine dialogue at a theological and philosophical level, being prepared as a Christian to seek Truth in the midst of open-ended debate. I enter such debate, declaring my loyalty to the uniqueness of God's revelation in Jesus Christ – else I would not be participating in the dialogue as a Christian – but I also put my own faith at risk each time I open myself to the faith of the other.

III

Living with other faiths, however, also involves dialogue at another and more common level, that of day to day living as I meet and engage with people of other faiths in the multifaith society that is contemporary Britian. Speaking personally, such dialogue serves to broaden the mind, deepen the understanding and enrich the quality of life beyond even the greatest imagination.

When I returned to live in Britain in the mid-seventies the sun was already well set on Empire, rising on the Commonwealth of Nations and beginning to dawn on the European Economic Community. The country was now decidedly multicultural, multiracial and multifaith. In mid–1976 the Office of Population Censuses and Surveys estimated a population of 1,771,000 'coloured people' for the United Kingdom as a whole and in January 1977 the Central Statistical Office projected a growth rate of 5 per cent in the next ten years – in other words, just under five out of every hundred people by the mid-eighties. Many of these people are of Afro-Caribbean descent and profess Christian faith while Jews and white British who convert to other faiths do not appear in such statistics. Race, culture and faith, it may seem obvious to observe, do not always coincide. More immediately relevant for the purpose of our present discussion are some educated guesses made by the British Council of Churches in January 1984.

There are probably some 800,000 Muslims – mainly from Pakistan and Bangladesh but also from parts of Africa and the Middle East. Hindus total around three to four hundred thousand with Leicester being the largest Hindu city, apart from Durban in South Africa, outside India. There are 200,000 Sikhs from the Punjab and East Africa; approximately 400,000 Jews and many thousands of Buddhists from the Chinese and Vietnamese communities. There are also smaller communities of Zoroastrians and Jains as well as a thriving Baha'i community.

The degree of religious observance, of course, is more difficult to assess.

Living with, mixing with, rubbing shoulders daily with – whether in actuality or through the media – people of other faiths in Britain today, even belonging to the same society, often evokes in me a sense of shame, attended, I hope, by a real repentance.

When I meet Jews I am reminded not just of Britain's anti–Nazi stance in the Second World War, but of the expulsion of the Jews from England under Edward I in 1290 and above all of the Holocaust. I think then of the Christian roots of anti-Semitism, of how easy it was for Christians to turn Jesus's openness to the Gentiles into a rejection of the Jews and to interpret the death of Jesus as due, not to the sinful nature of all humankind but specifically to the sin of the Jewish people. Of course there are other roots of anti-Semitism but Christianity as a religion must shoulder its share of the blame.

When I meet Rastafarians I am reminded not just of William Wilberforce and the movement for the abolition of slavery, motivated as it was by Christian values, nor even of the Church's stance against apartheid in South Africa today, but of how the institutions of slavery and apartheid have prospered in Christian lands. I think then of how Christians have used the bible to justify both. I recall in particular that the Boers of South Africa saw themselves mirrored in the Old

Testament: God's chosen, an Exodus people, making their way through the desert to the promised land, rejecting black people as the cursed race of Ham and settling in their lands as allotted them by God.

When I meet Muslims I am reminded not just of renascent Islam on the march nor even of the past glories of Islamic art and science but of the inglorious Crusades. I recall how the Crusaders of 1099 massacred the Jewish and Muslim inhabitants of Jerusalem while in 1187 the Muslim Saladin proved magnanimous in his treatment of the city's Christian defenders; also of the persecution of Muslims in Spain under the Catholic monarchs, Ferdinand and Isabella.

When I meet Hindus from an East African background I am reminded not just of their business acumen and strong cultural identity but of the arrogant, civilizing, Christian imperialism which recruited coolies for the Uganda Railway, uprooting them from their homeland without due care or forethought for their future well-being. Such an establishment would not have cared to foresee the coming of African independence and the welcome accorded its colonial citizens by a reluctant motherland.

And so I could go on, endlessly cataloguing the failures of history in interfaith relationships, hanging my head in shame and muttering words of repentance. But, happily, there is another side to the story, not in small measure due to the capacity of people on all sides to forgive and forget. Thus I can instead begin to experience and enjoy the richness and diversity of customs and cultures which people of other races and other faiths have brought to Britain, at times making and expressing certain reservations but always seeking to be tolerant and understanding.

I go into an Indian restaurant, taking with me a friend who is a vegetarian. I am reminded by the variety of vegetable dishes available of the doctrine of non-violence and Hindu reverence for life in all its forms.

I attend a Hindu wedding and I recall the stability of many Indian arranged marriages because each partner enters the relationship intending to grow in love.

I take a group of students to visit the local mosque and come away with a fresh understanding of and renewed commitment to prayer. And I recall the rich discourse on the interior life which I heard delivered in a Nairobi mosque, the deep devotion of ordinary Muslims as they broke the fast of Ramadan.

I listen to Rabbi Lionel Blue as he gives his thought for the day on Radio 4 and I begin to appreciate again the things that are good about family life and close-knit community living for there is a sense of sanctity about a Jewish home.

And I meet a youthful member of a new religious movement on the street – a saffron-robed devotee of Hare Krishna or a fund-raising Moonie – and I am reminded of the spiritual bankruptcy of much of Western culture, even of what passes for Christianity. I also want to re-affirm the importance of hard-won religious freedoms.

I join a women's group and, confronted by feminist unease with the place and role of women in most of the world's religions, I must face honestly what has become for many secular humanists today a major stumbling-block to religious belief of any kind. As a Christian, I must recall that although, for his time, Jesus may have had an enlightened approach to women and Paul may have declared the equality of the sexes in his great manifesto on Christian liberty, the Church for the greater part of its history has denied women full human personhood. And as a respecter of other faiths, even after making some allowance for cultural factors, I must admit that on the whole Jewish, Muslim, Hindu and numerous other cumulative traditions allow even less dignity and equality to women.

At present I hold the position of a diocesan missioner in the Church of England. And you are entitled to ask how I can engage in mission and at the same time with integrity enter into dialogue with people of other faiths.

But I make no apologies. In Christian theology mission is God's mission. God sent Jesus into the world. So too all Christians are sent – I am sent – to be instruments of God's unconditional love for the world. My identity as a Christian is inextricably bound up with love for God and love for the neighbour. And that neighbour may be a member of a faith other than Christian, a person who needs to be embraced with the warmth of love in the midst of a cold, unwelcoming and perhaps even racist society. In Jesus Christ I believe I see and experience that love most fully manifest and I wish to share it with others. Jesus it is who constrains me to give the fabled drink of cold water in his name.

Finally, who am I, a simple believer, ultimately to perceive the economy of a God who presides over a world in which, although Christians have sought for almost two thousand years to proclaim the gospel worldwide, Hindus and Buddhists predominate in two of the most populous of its lands, Muslims continue to increase, the so-called primal religions re-emerge and new religious movements rise and decline like the waxing and waning of the moon? There may be only one God; but God has many names. Similarly, God works not only in and through the Church but by the Spirit in the world. Moreover, God's ways are mysterious ways, to be followed but not always to be fathomed.

MARTIN ISRAEL

Martin Israel is the priest of Holy Trinity with All Saints in South Kensington and a consultant pathologist at the Royal College of Surgeons. Brought up in South Africa in the Jewish faith he is now at home in the mystical Christian tradition, believing that God is central to all human life and demands total commitment from his believers.

He is widely known as a counsellor and conductor of religious retreats and has written many books on the spiritual life, including "Summons to Life", "Precarious Living", "The Pain that Heals", "The Spirit of Counsel" and "Living Alone".

The Discipline of Love

There is no word bandied about more thoughtlessly than love: it appears regularly in fiction, the media of mass communication, political propaganda and private conversation, to say nothing of addresses in religious assemblies of all denominations. When loosely used it seems to denote an irresistible attraction of one person to another, but there are unspoken undertones of possession and subjugation. When a child says he loves chocolates, he is speaking more truly than he knows about the typical love of the marketplace: just as the chocolate is consumed by the child's appetite, so is the object of worldly love used in an unconsciously predatory way by the other person. Neither the lover nor the beloved grows in the transaction, and in the end both are gradually sucked into the vortex of possessiveness that is miscalled love. It appears that all too often human love is essentially a destructive infatuation that wanes as another object of affection appears. Even if the affection is sincere and longlasting, it tends to envelop both parties in a web of selfishness that closes on a note of mute tragedy when death claims one of the partners. The love of the marketplace is in fact usually a feeling of affection, passionate or transient as the case may be, that is selfish and shows little concern for the welfare of the greater community. It is often predatory and nearly always remarkably blind.

Nevertheless, love is at the heart of true spirituality, especially the Christian variety. In the bible we are exhorted to love our neighbour as ourselves; Jesus in the immortal parable of the good Samaritan extends the understanding of the neighbour to include all people in our vicinity, indeed all the world. What then is the essential difference between Christian love and the love of the marketplace? The answer is that all true love, whether of the marketplace or the Christian assembly, has a common origin and end, but whereas the well-meaning atheist has no understanding, no deeper grasp of the source of that love, the Christian hails that source with reverence and thanksgiving. The Christian knows that all love comes from God, and that our love is a response to his: we love because he loved us first. As soon as we begin to know God as a living presence within our lives, we cease to look after our own interests to the exclusion of all else, and work instead in service to our fellow creatures, so that they too may begin to know God's love. The end of that love is the growth of the individual to true personhood, a state of being fully revealed in Jesus of Nazareth, who is the proper person. A Christian would affirm this supremacy of Jesus above all the other great spiritual leaders of the human race, but without in any way denigrating these others, by virtue not only of his teaching but also his life of healing, transforming, and above all his absolute self-sacrifice even to his own appalling death on the cross. He, above all others, shows us by his life the nature of the unseen God. Furthermore, as a result of this self-giving even to death, he bequeaths to those around him, inadequate as they are – and indeed as we all are – through their treachery and self-seeking, a new understanding of reality. They begin to grasp that real happiness does not consist in getting as much as possible for themselves, but rather in giving themselves for the greater good of all around them. The end of this self-giving is that the world itself may be raised from the darkness of vice and hatred to the light of a purpose that can harness the wonderful human potential of creative activity and love for all its creatures. This purpose goes beyond mortal life, and is of the nature of eternity, for our life on earth is a mere parenthesis in the greater life ahead of all of us. The idea of eternity is indeed common to all types of spirituality, seeing our mortal life embraced in a realm of meaning and love that transcends death. Eternity is the experience of the nature of God; it transcends time, which is the medium of the growth of the person into his destined form, even the stature of Christ himself.

The Christian religion envisages a tremendous destiny for the human race, created in God's image and through the travail of humiliation, loss and death to grow fully into that image as revealed by Jesus himself. But at the heart of us all

167

there is a flaw which tends to attract us to the realms of selfish gratification rather than the risen life of service and love for our fellow creatures. This flaw seems to be an inevitable result of the free will that God has bestowed on us; he has given us the wonderful power to decide for ourselves, but when we choose the lesser selfishness over the greater common good, our own interests above those of our neighbours, pain and suffering ensue, which, if left unchecked, could encompass our own destruction and finally that of the entire world. It is the realisation of this flaw that makes our constant contact with God imperative: we of ourselves move irresistibly into succumbing to the temptations of self-seeking and the tumultuous satisfaction of our lusts. It is only when we are attached to that which transcends ourselves and unites us one to another that a higher concern may dominate our consciousness.

That of which I speak is God; neither to be named nor defined, let alone described, he is known to ourselves when we are quiet and can give of ourselves to the present moment in absolute awareness. In other words, we know God best when we are still and attentive: a presence fills our being, and we are intuitively aware of a power and a love that cannot be grasped let alone delineated. And yet that burning presence gives us a personal, subjective, yet certain awareness of meaning which brings warmth and purpose to our present situation, to our endeavours in the shadow of eternity. Thus it comes about that the first three great commandments of the Ten Commandments concern our relationship with the nameless yet intensely personal, loving God. We are to have none beside him, to worship him alone and not any created idol, and to hold his name in awe so that we never misuse it. It is a fact that until we know God and can enjoy his presence wherever we may be and at all times, our desires can never be lifted up above purely personal gratification; even if they are satisfied, we move inexorably towards that death which obliterates the body and all its senses. There can be no full understanding of love until we move beyond the domination of the senses to the One who is eternal and brings all life into eternal consciousness by the power of love.

It follows therefore that the essential spiritual act is prayer.

This is not to be seen so much as a conversation with God as a raising of the entire will to him. Prayer has been defined as the ascent of the mind to God; it is also the communion (or fellowship) of the soul with God. In that state of wordless communion which is called contemplation, we may listen to what God is saying to us in the depths of our being rather than simply chatter to him. Most human conversation is in fact idle chatter, in which we are much more interested in unburdening ourselves to those around us than in listening in silence to what they have to tell us. We may have to reach the situation of the prodigal son, destitute among the pigs, before we can be absolutely silent and hear what the Holy Spirit is telling us. Here in fact we come to the root of the difference between the sincere secular concern of the marketplace (to be contrasted with the sensuality and selfishness of much human intercourse) and the love of the committed Christian. The concerned secularist knows what is best for those in need, and proceeds to enact legislation to put matters aright. He is in charge, and unconsciously assumes a god-like role (in this respect a god can be defined as any focus of independent will, and as such the word is used on a number of occasions in the book of Psalms). But humans, even at their most brilliant, are poor gods, being subject to their own prejudices and weaknesses. These are aspects of the flaw in the personality already mentioned. People tend to be manipulative even when they have the best will in the world; they tend to treat those they are endeavouring to help as little children incapable of any rational decision of their own. As the learned, concerned ones impose their wills on others, so does resentment arise, and in the end all is consumed in bitterness and futility.

By contrast, the Christian who is true to his Master, will submit his will to God's scrutiny in deep prayer. He will learn humility, and attain the wonderful quality of being able to enter into the deeper life of the person he is trying to help, just as Jesus entered into the lives of the people around him, uttering words of healing rather than judgement. To be sure, the process of inner cleansing through prayer takes a long time, and many Christians young in their faith are also full of dogmatic certainty and insensitive advice. They tend to have a rather naive view of the workings of the Holy Spirit, failing to disentangle his presence from their own background prejudices, and so become unconsciously manipulative like their secular counterparts. But as time goes by, they too learn greater wisdom and humility, and then the help they afford to many others both in their actions and their intercessions can be life-transforming. In our lives on earth we all have to manoeuvre ourselves between the two extremes of activism and quietism: the former is obsessed with human activity in all social issues, and has above all else to be seen doing something, whereas the latter leaves it all to God, whom we serve only by prayer. At present the Church is excessively activist, being greatly concerned in various social and international issues with almost the assurance of professional politicians and social workers. This is all to the good, provided the Church does not lose its spiritual discernment in the pursuit of the immediate millenium. It should remember that God was in Christ reconciling the world to himself. Change must be accompanied by the love of reconciliation and not the hatred of human judgement.

On the other hand, no Christian should remain oblivious of any social injustice or human suffering. The parable of the good Samaritan leaves us in no doubt where our duty lies. It is interesting that in this story, while the professional religious agents passed by the man in need, the outcast Samaritan, who was really outside the pale, ran to help him. It seems that the pain of rejection made the Samaritan much more aware of the hurt man than were the priest and Levite. Once we have suffered in the school of life we can put ourselves with greater alacrity into another man's shoes; by contrast, ritual religious worship devoid of a deeper base can easily deaden our sense of compassion. This was the reproach levelled against the Church in the past, and not without reason. Thus prayer activates our social response but does not replace it. Our lives are an amalgam of divine grace and human free will; the one is not more important than the other, but the grace of God precedes and informs the will that then has to get on with the work.

Idolatry is the great temptation in our lives. What we lay the greatest stress upon, what the heart vibrates to most passionately is where our loyalty lies. "Where your treasure is, there shall your heart be also" (Matthew 6:21). In Christ, whose life is an image of the divine nature, our treasure is firmly fixed on God, and in him resides our heart. Therefore our attention is no longer fixed on the goods of this world, whether they be money, status, power, personal gifts of intellect or beauty, or even another person, wonderful as our relationship with him or her may be.

Once we know God as Father, revealed in the life of his Son Jesus, we can put worldly things into proper perspective. The Christian life is not other-worldly, indeed the Word became flesh and partook fully of this world with us; on the contrary, it sees all earthly things in their form as eternal manifestations of God. Therefore neither money nor power, status nor reputation, personal gifts nor human relationships are bad in themselves, indeed they are all God's gifts to us, but they have to be seen in perspective. They are here to be used, enjoyed and also ennobled, just as the priest consecrates the elements, the bread and wine, of the Eucharist. It is when they take hold of our lives that they assume a demonic character. On the other hand, the things of this world take on an even greater splendour when they are seen to be the unique creation of God; instead of using them thoughtlessly, we begin to appreciate their intrinsic beauty and cherish them. Of nothing is this more true than human relationships. In fact, the last part of the Ten Commandments is taken up with proper relationships with our neighbours. We are enjoined to pay special respect to our parents, whose burden it is to give us nurture and education during our years of helplessness, remembering the essential formative role the parent plays in the lives of his offspring. This is a far cry from the promiscuity in relationships that is such a common feature of contemporary secular life.

Indeed, the problem of sex is probably the predominant one in any secular society. The sexual drive is very powerful, being aimed at the survival of the race – "be fruitful and multiply" is the divine injunction to the patriarchs at the beginning of the Judeo-Christian sacred history. At present, however, over-population is one of the most urgent problems confronting the human species; to some extent it has been counteracted by the availability of contraceptive agents recommended in most advanced societies. Now therefore, at least in the developed countries, sexual intercourse can take place as often as desired without any rational embargo, apart from the danger of venereal diseases, which, with the advent of Aids, poses an ever-increasing threat to many people. Nevertheless, in most societies people take extramarital intercourse for granted, while the statistics for marital breakdown escalate violently. In counselling work it is almost a relief to encounter a person who is happily married or to see a well united family.

What has Christian spirituality to say to this sorry state of affairs? It affirms the divine creation of man, and indeed of all the world, laying special stress on human rationality which allows us to cooperate with God and carry out his work in the world. It is in this spirit that the statement that we were created in God's image is best understood. It also affirms the sacred nature of human relationships, especially the deep inner communion that attends sexual intercourse, which is a sacrament of God's love for us. Therefore this act is a uniquely special one, and should not be undertaken until there is abiding love in the partners and not merely superficial affection. This love has a responsible, executive function, being concerned about the welfare of the other person, a responsibility that does not end with the cessation of the coitus. The proof of that love is a solemn undertaking to protect one another in the future, indeed to the end of life on earth. To this end there is the beautiful but awesome marriage ceremony, which cements the union till death parts husband and wife. There is to be fidelity between the marriage partners of such purity that the inroads of adultery are impossible. Only when a marriage is founded on love and erected on service, preferably adorned by an emerging family, does the threat of adultery evaporate. Fidelity is essential both for the growth into trust of both partners and for the good of the children. As the couple learn to accept one another more and more, so they can accept their neighbours more fully also. The command to honour our parents is a by-product of a healthy, loving family life; once adultery and divorce cast their shadows, the united family disintegrates and the offspring are trapped in divided loyalties. In the contemporary type of ménage without marriage, the man or woman can depart summarily, so that the children are left members of a one-parent family. What parent deserves honour in these circumstances? And what is the future of the children, deprived of the support and stability of loving family life?

It would be a serious omission in this respect to evade the question of homosexuality, which since the liberalising legislation of the sixties has become more open and clamant as many people seem to be this way orientated. Among secular agencies homosexuality is now taken as a matter of course, and in many societies special centres have been set up for the assistance of homosexuals. There is a strong Christian disapproval of this way of life, based on stern biblical prohibitions, but it has to be faced that many homosexuals are deeply spiritual people with strong Christian commitment. One way out of the difficulty is obviously continence and celibacy, but it is increasingly recognised that deep love can occur between two people of the same sex, and that a coldly prohibitive attitude can be sadly destructive to the personal growth of the individuals. Therefore there are special Christian agencies also available to give expert counsel. The essential Christian prerequisite for all relationships is love, which is, as St Paul writes, "patient, kind and non-envious. It does not boast, nor is it conceited, rude, selfish or quick to take offence. It keeps no score of wrongs, nor does it gloat over other men's sins, but delights in the truth. There is nothing it cannot face, there is no limit to its faith, its hope, and its endurance. Love will never come to an end." (I Corinthians 13: 4–8).

Promiscuous relationships, whether heterosexual or homosexual, are to be strongly condemned; apart from their spiritual debasement, they are very likely to be complicated by venereal diseases. Where there is true love in the Pauline sense between two people, we should wait with bated breath and give thanks to God. We know too little to give judgement, which in any case is reserved for God. It should finally be said that the modern obsession with genital sex generally is not a good thing, unless it were to be argued cynically that coitus is preferable to violence and war. If people were more orientated to prayer, their communion with God would temper their sexual desires without in any way neutralising them. Sex is much more than genital union; it is an essential way of communication between one person and another. The true celibate combines within himself or herself the elements of both sexes in such harmony that he or she emanates a completeness that does not need anyone else to add to it. Such a person is equally happy alone or with people, not needing the company of others nor, on the other hand, rejecting it. The true celibate is at the service of humanity at large, and does not require rewards.

The other great problem in human life is the tendency to violence, whether murder, stealing or character-assassination that shows itself in giving false evidence against our neighbour. This may take the form of malicious gossip so that the person's reputation is subtly and irrevocably impugned. The key to much violence is the absence of love in our lives, which in turn is a reflection of the deprivation of love that we suffered when we were children. I can never love my neighbour until I learn to love myself; if I am mean to myself, I shall certainly not be generous to my neighbour. Hence we are told to love our neighbours as ourselves. To prevent the evil of such violent behaviour as killing, stealing, and maligning others there is first of all the deterrent approach of punishment, even of death for murder. The Law of Moses proscribes wrong-doers in no uncertain fashion, ordering the penalty of death for numerous offences, including murder and adultery. As spiritual consciousness matures, such violent responses to crimes are tempered with mercy, and Jesus tells us to love our enemies and pray for those who persecute us (Matthew 5:44). He tells us furthermore not to set ourselves against the man who wrongs us (Matthew 5: 39). One must, in all due realism, object that to behave thus in our contemporary violent society would be to court disaster. In many urban areas it is most unwise to leave churches open to the public if there is nobody present to keep order, for they are sure to be desecrated. Nevertheless, Jesus's injunctions are quite right: until there is a change in our own hearts there will never be a change in the perspective of either our local community or of the world generally. We personally can move beyond the temptation to kill, steal, and lie about other people only as we are more fixed in God in prayer. As we have already noted, it is the love of God that makes worldly possessions and powers increasingly unnecessary. A critic might argue with considerable justification that the Christian Church itself has not been particularly immune from the temptation to aggrandisement and power politics through the centuries; indeed, it has been the agent of much violence and cruelty both to deviants within its own ranks and to the Jews. This is always the result of linking physical power with spiritual authority; the temptation to world domination is irresistible. This after all was the nature of Jesus's third temptation in the wilderness, when the devil offered him all the kingdoms of the world on condition that he fell down and did him homage. If only the Church had been faithful to God in prayer it would never have fallen victim to the urge for power! Today it is largely irrelevant in many societies, even of the Western world.

As we enter more fully into the Christian way, so love tempers our desire for revenge, our lust for justice on an eye for an eye, a tooth for a tooth basis. While in no way blinding ourselves to the safety of the community and the necessity for tough penal measures against hardened criminals, we look more towards their rehabilitation and less towards their interminable punishment. The abolition of capital punishment is always to be welcomed in a community; amongst the undeveloped nations it is clearly impractical, for stern deterrence is essential for elementary public safety, but in more developed societies it points to a more responsible attitude to all its members, the good and the bad alike, all of whom are children of God. While some criminals seem to be 'evil geniuses', in the same way that we have spiritual geniuses, musical geniuses and mathematical geniuses, for whom nothing apparently can be done apart from rigorous permanent segregation, most are the products of terrible backgrounds where there was virtually no love. They were at least as much sinned against as sinning, and there is always the hope of their partial rehabilitation at the hands of a sympathetic probation service.

On the other hand, the Christian witness is never permissive. It has definite standards based on the teachings of scripture and the platonic valuation of goodness (or love), truth and beauty as the way of the intellect to God. While it may forgive perverse behaviour, it never condones it, because of the high valuation it holds of the human personality. We are God's children, created in his image, and are ultimately "to escape the corruption with which lust has infected the world, and come to share in the very being of God".

Every action has its fruits, the law of cause and effect works relentlessly throughout our lives both in this world and the next. Therefore only the highest standards will suffice. But transcending all this is the love of God which has been infused into human consciousness. As St Paul says, love is the fulfilling of the Law. St Paul came to see that although the Law proscribed various sins, it was impotent in helping the sinner to lead a new life. It was the advent of Christ into the world that made God's grace freely available to all who had faith in him, and then a new mind was born that could enter the dimension of spiritual life. What the naked human will could not achieve was made possible by the love of God made tangible in his son. But we have to be constantly open to that love, for we too at any moment can slip back into the old ways. Our will can alone fulfil the change offered us in Christ.

EDWARD BAILEY

Edward Bailey is Rector of Winterbourne parish in Bristol and runs the Network for the Study of Implicit Religion, an organisation he set up several years ago. In 1968 he began researching into popular religious beliefs and coined the phrase 'implicit religion' to denote a sphere of personal meanings and values which he believes play a powerful role in peoples' lives. He wrote a doctorate on the implicit religion of his local parishioners which drew heavily on observations gathered while working as a barman in the village public house.

He believes that there is a value-system symbolized by the word 'Christianity' which people in this country adhere to – and occasionally achieve – and that it is his task as a priest to inspire this implicit Christian faith rather than to dictate the doctrines of the Church.

The Religion of the People

'I believe in Christianity,' parents will tell me when we discuss the christening of their child. And if a set of core beliefs or creeds were drawn together from the religious beliefs of the nation I am sure this statement would be paramount, vying only with 'I believe in God' for primacy.

It is popular to talk about the great collapse in religious belief – secularisation – in this country, harking back to a golden age when the theological principles of Christianity were imprinted on the hearts of the people. What we do have evidence for, however, is a doggedly persistent faith in 'Christianity', not seen as a set of dogmas but as symbolizing an intrinsic faith or spirit. It is this 'Christianity' which I come across daily as a priest. I believe it represents a kind of religion – being the major manifestation of a divinity. So it should be treated with the utmost sensitivity and reverence.

This faith in 'Christianity' reveals itself most clearly in the widespread desire for infant baptism. It is usually the father who articulates the basic doctrinal affirmation: 'I believe in Christianity.' The mother will nod in agreement. His feelings are better summarised, in the words of the Church's thanksgiving: "All things come from you and of your own do we give you."

If the parents were asked bleakly, 'Why do you want your child baptised?', each would offer a different reason – though both would share the same faith in this religious act. The father might think of the child's future and try to specify the purpose and desired effect of the ceremony. The mother would be more likely to respond in a theologically pragmatic way, 'So he'll be alright if anything happens'.

These particular statements are part of a wider philosophy – a religious faith – which emerges on occasions like these. It can be summarised in a form based on that of the Moslem creed:

I believe in Christianity
I insist on the right of everyone to make up his own mind,
And I affirm the value of values.

This pronouncement about Christianity is truly a confession of faith, comparable to a confession of sin. They may not have articulated it before – in the sense of being put into words or brought together – but they are not making it up.

It is, of course, possible to be sceptical of the thoughts of parents wanting infant baptism for their child. Twenty years ago, some parish clergy thought that people would do anything to have their baby baptised. They would even do something, temporarily, such as attending a course of instruction or coming to church for a few weeks. But, they said, it made no difference afterwards. The parents seemed to have done nothing about the Christian upbringing of their older children – so far as public worship or mutual learning or private prayer were concerned. They sometimes openly stated that they had no intention of doing anything more specific for this child beyond sending him to Sunday School if someone else provided it, at a convenient time and place. Neither they nor the godparents had been confirmed, or would think of confirming their own baptism now. Especially when it came to Sunday mornings, it always seemed to be Mammon (or, perhaps, self) in some form, that won.

Naturally, it was concluded, they would tell the vicar what they thought he wanted to hear; and, as charity believeth all things, he had no option but to give them the benefit of the doubt and hope for the best, whatever his own faith-less prognosis might suggest. The two parties sometimes seemed, at least to the would-be realist, like partners in some mutual confidence-trick.

However, a blanket cynicism, especially one that is convinced of its own realism, runs the risk of discouraging the very discovery or revelation that would bring its own validity into question. We do not have to abdicate our own understanding of baptism, or of Christianity; but, as Lord Acton said, we have no right to disagree with a critic until we can argue his own case for him – better, even, than he can himself.

Simply to list the limitations in the parents' commitment is an inevitable counsel of despair. It also runs the risk of arrogance, of limiting the sphere of God's activity to our understanding of it. What is required, first, is a matching care, in teasing out what this ceremony, upon which so many set such great store, does mean for them. Afterwards we may make such comparisons as we wish.

Very occasionally the parents will say they want their baby baptised so he'll be able to get married in church. It is probably also in the mind of some who do not mention it. The reference appears to be to the building; to church with a small 'c' so to speak. However, this runs the risk of imposing an imported distinction upon undifferentiated data. To the speaker, the building may be seen as containing a clergyman who represents the Church as a community which tries to convey something of the spirit of Christ. To be married in church, therefore, may, indicate a loyalty to all that the Church is seen as standing for.

For the great majority of parents, however, their first reason is, 'so he'll be a member of the Church.' Sometimes this is phrased, in keeping with the contemporary emphasis upon individual subjectivity, 'so he'll feel he's a member of the Church'. As a single-sentence summary of the desired effects of baptism, it anticipates the Church of England's current ritual: "We therefore welcome you into the Lord's family." While no one sentence can list all the possible deductions, or combine all the traditional descriptions, its more subjective re-phrasing also echoes the association of the rite, in the New Testament, with the gift of the Spirit, incorporating the individual into Christ. Indeed, the popular attachment to the description of baptism as christening, emphasising the official bestowal of a personal name upon the newly-born individual, reflects the understanding of baptism as the gift of new identity, and the beginning of growth into a mature new life. The parallel may be unselfconscious, but truth can be taught without a tutor.

The second reason given by the great majority of the parents is, 'so he'll be able to make up his own mind for himself when he's older'. Logically, this may seem to contradict the earlier motive, for there is no particular moment, and no way, in which either the parents or the organisation expects and enables the baptised to renounce his membership of the Church. The sacrament, appropriately described as something 'done', can never be undone, and neither party has any desire that it should be. The parents, however, see confirmation as intended to provide the opportunity for the individual to confirm his own baptism for himself.

In view of the procedure and explanation of the Church of England, at least since its rationalisation in the last century, this understanding of confirmation is by no means illogical. Indeed, the clergy may be interested to note how widely their practice and teaching have been grasped. In particular, its emphasis upon the decision-making element, within the total consciousness of individuals, stems from the Victorian stress upon this strand within the tradition.

Whether or not the two main motives for baptism are compatible with each other, many of the parents were recognised by many of the clergy as being sincere both in their desire for baptism for their baby, and in their profession of belief in (what they understood by) Christianity. Faith, even if blind, is not necessarily feigned. The difference between the two parties did not lie so much in their commitment to the ritual or to its overall effect, or even to the association of baptism with being Christian. It lay in the precise content of the commitment, and, especially, in the manner of expressing it. The child, as both cause for thanksgiving and advent of responsibility, put the parents in mind of the simple profundities they had touched upon in the story of Christmas, and at Sunday School. They valued those memories, and what they represented. Their nostalgia, and accompanying desire to make it part of their own child's future memories, were real. Indeed, the Church is well-versed in the ability of remembrance to re-present past events in spirit and in truth.

Whether or not the reasons for, and understanding of, baptism were compatible with the current perceptions of tradition, is another question again. Yet it is hardly to be expected that the meaning of the rite in twentieth-century Britain will be identical with its meaning in the Mediterranean world of the first century. Indeed, much of what the New Testament teaches about its meaning was only written because it did not appear to mean all of this to some of those who had already been baptised. Similarly, it should not be expected to mean the same to all, even of those who have undergone the rite, today. It is one of the functions of a sacrament or covenant, as of the incarnation and atonement, to unite what might appear opposite: to redeem their variety, without destroying their diversity.

The beliefs which emerge at an infant baptism are no different from any other symbol, in gaining much of their meaning from the immediate context. Thus, a group that is large and formal may need to begin by calling upon God, or even Providence: only when the human spirit has come to the fore can 'we ask Jesus'. Similarly, where human consciousness emphasises what is internal and invisible, as in contemporary society, there is a proper sense in which religion, even the Christian religion, is in part both individual and private. So there is suspicion of those who wear their hearts on their sleeves, and support for such sayings as 'Actions speak louder than words', 'Still waters run deep', 'Empty vessels make the most noise'. In this social context, the statement of a personal commitment, to what is largely seen as a moral ideal, carries an unusual authority.

It is, first and foremost, a description of the self: *I* believe. It is comparable with, I love (you). Such statements may subsequently be made public, with the assistance of such rituals as baptism and marriage services. Should a clergyman reject a request for baptism, in this light a deep sense of dejection may follow.

Turning from beliefs expressed at baptisms, we need to ask what is meant by 'Christianity'. Such brief epithets can speak volumes: an entire stance for living is encapsulated in mutually recognised formulae such as Hinduism or the Buddha, Israel, Christ or Islam. Their simplicity may belie a contrast that extends even to their categories.

In this case, the belief in 'Christianity' is not simply belief in Christ. It is true that he plays a part in the 'Christianity' that is believed in. The verbal similarity is more than a matter of etymology in the antiquarian sense. For it is constantly being fed and maintained by the Church, along with many other agencies with differing motives.

For some who are active in the life of the Church, the part played by Christ as a living contemporary is personally important. His company is probably central to the devotion of the considerable number of women who say they often pray while washing up. However, most of those who follow this creed describe themselves as believing in Christianity, rather than in Christ. In the last analysis, his historicity is comparable to that of Krishna: he is of cultural, not cosmic significance. His title is a respectful surname (as sometimes in the New Testament). Ultimately, the belief is in a spiritual ethic, rather than an individual; a generalised, heavenly Son of Man, rather than a citizen-carpenter; a myth that sanctifies flesh and blood, rather than a being of flesh and blood, mythically understood. Awareness concentrates upon his ministry, rather than his death or resurrection. He is an example, even a Saviour; but he inspires, rather than cures.

Neither is the belief in 'Christianity' simply a belief in God. God plays a part in this world-view, and in this living faith. To some, including some who have little or nothing to do with the community of those active in the Church, he is real, his presence is near, and his care is certain. However, although their awareness of him may not be shared, even with their own spouse, they are probably a small minority.

For most, God is a part of the 'Christianity' that is believed in: as the backcloth, he is part of the theatre, but without being the centre of attention. He is the *sine qua non* of the drama, an essential part of the whole, the keystone of the arch; but he is not the primary object of belief. Just as this is not the faith of the writers in the New Testament, neither is it that of the Old Testament (that is, at its most characteristic). He may overlook sin (as in some views of the atonement), but he has no opportunity to express forgiveness of it.

Nor is the belief in 'Christianity' a belief in the Church. The Church is an important element in the 'Christianity' that is believed in. Indeed, sometimes it is also said to be believed in. However, it is never identified with 'Christianity': it is only human. The myth was only ever fully realised in Jesus.

If the Church is believed in, it is as a vehicle of 'Christianity', keeping it alive, supporting its adherents in a Christian way; or as a witness to 'Christianity', teaching its message, advertising its virtues, and appealing for converts. The belief in the Church is dependent upon the prior and primary belief in Christianity.

So Christianity is the god, spirit or ethos from whom it is hoped real help for the world (salvation) can come. Christ, God, and the Church are its three main elements, but they remain its faces, its personae. An eschatological sense of time and triumph exist in contemporary society: but they have little connection with faith in this Christianity. Christ is a phenomenon of this culture: his superiority is tied to its superiority. In the last analysis, his historicity is immaterial, like Krishna's. What matters is the moral influence of the ideal he symbolises. All religions are usually the same: the idea appeals, not because of any claim to knowledge, but because it reflects an ideal state of affairs.

Positively, then, this 'Christianity' would be described as a way of life, or as a value-system. It is a way of life that is summarised, anachronistically, as the Ten Commandments or the Sermon on the Mount; or in the oft-quoted parable of helping a little old lady across the road. Such explanations are to be understood as referring to general witnesses to its spirit, rather than as precise descriptions; as another Christian may say that be believes in the bible or the Church.

Commitment to this philosophy is sometimes justified as though it were part of a random, but global, insurance policy: 'You never know, I might want help myself one day.' However, that is an unconvincing attempt at rationalisation, along the ritualised tram-lines of the current utilitarian mass culture. Its truer authority lies in an intuitive conviction, widespread but private, that others matter, as I do. This is the ontological and ethical ground of the contemporary appeal of, and to, human rights. This apprehension is religious in character. It unites belief in with belief that, appropriate response with accepted reality; moral law and natural law, person and universe.

It is this apprehension that accounts for the public's desire for religious education in schools. Positively, it accounts for

'Christianity's' determined insistence on measuring the reality of professed belief in God, by the reality of concern for others. Negatively, it accounts for 'Christianity's' apparent unconcern with Christ's first commandment, and its elevation into first place of his second commandment.

So a rationalisation that comes closer to the existential belief in 'Christianity', might run:

Everyone has to have a value-system;
'Christianity' is the best value-system available;
Christ, God and the Church stand for 'Christianity'.

As an object of commitment, 'Christianity' may appear somewhat vague. This by no means makes it unique among commitments. The objects of faith or love, God or the beloved, always defeat description. Indeed, were it otherwise, the depth and width of the commitment might be suspect. Specific descriptions, and developed doctrines, can only arise when the object is distanced. Their absence indicates a commitment which is more subjective, less easy to externalise; a theme of, but within, one's own life, rather than an object of some kind outside it.

An affirmation which is at the heart of popular belief in Christianity is the well-known saying, 'You don't have to go to church to be a Christian'. In other words, worship does not guarantee either the possession or production of 'Christianity'. It's all right for those who like that sort of thing because, if it is not done for show, then it is well-meant and harmless. Indeed, it is a service to society, because someone must keep things going. But to go for the wrong reasons, when you don't feel like it, could be not only personally inconvenient, but also counter-productive, so far as Christianity is concerned. You could emerge worse, spiritually, than when you went in.

Almost as common, thirdly, is a catena of sayings about not mixing politics with religion. Again, it is possible to see historical origins for such a belief, in the Reformation, in fear of ecclesiastical domination, and in suspicion of Romish plots. Certainly these are maintained by some text-books, occasional sacerdotalism, and explanations of Bonfire Night.

Yet these are probably charter-myths, rather than reasons: they legitimise, rather than create, such attitudes. They are the religious form of the care that is taken to ensure that 'no-one's going to tell me what to do'. There is a determination that no functionary – religious, political, or economic – should combine too many roles. For the identity of the individual is to be found in the gaps between the specialised expectations. There is a deep determination to reserve unorganised spaces in society and in time, in order to preserve the ultimate sacred object – the self.

Mention of the self as the ultimate manifestation of sacredness within 'Christianity's' universe may sound more like a form of Hinduism than of Christianity, at least as the Church has conceived it. No doubt this is both a cause and effect of the absence of any positive word in ordinary English to describe that immense amount of pastoral care that is taken of the self: there is only 'selfish'. Certainly there is a great gulf between the faith of the people, and the official, if not conventional, faith of the Church.

This gulf is readily illustrated by looking in the English Hymnal for any hymn on the theme of Christ's second commandment. Yet the English Hymnal is one of the most widely-used hymn books in the Church of England, where the faith of the people might have been expected to find some kind of recognition.

However, it may also be suggested that there is just as great a gulf between the faith of the people and secular humanism. This gulf is apparent in the different use of the key word 'human'. For the British Humanist Association, the human is in distinction to the divine; so to be a Humanist is to bolster the substitution of the one for the other. For 'Christianity', and in popular usage, on the other hand, the human is only human. It is universally fallible, naturally errant, and hopelessly inadequate. But it is also loveable, and so forgiven. It is child-like, appealing because it invites us to become God-like. 'Tell Georgie he's a very naughty kitten, and that we love him very much.'

The God-like 'Christianity', to which there is such commitment, then, is a spiritual phenomenon. Its own deity is the self; or, lest that be misunderstood, selves. Morals are its sacraments: neither more nor less. It has been suggested that at the Reformation, English religion passed straight from the mystical to the moral, without ever being sacramental or theological in the Mediterranean or Teutonic manner. To be dogmatic or doctrinal, a fanatic or bigot, to fall for a panacea or messiah, are its vices. To see one's own self in perspective, demonstrated by the ability to laugh at oneself, is the relevant way to avoid idolatry. Thus the Great Train Robbers were cheeky and unfortunate enough to be caught, comedians rather than criminals. Though no Robin Hoods, their originality and relative success in 'beating the system' was heroic.

So the fundamental dichotomy of 'Christianity' is not between God and man, or law and spirit, or reason and emotion, or works and grace, or mature and immature. It is more nearly between the conscience and the flesh. That, however, is the experienced cause of conflict. The basic distinction is between good, in the sense of loving, and bad, in the sense of harming (the self or other selves).

Clearly, this, is one kind of Christianity; as village Hinduism is one kind of Hinduism; and as ecclesiastical Christianity, and philosophical Hinduism, are other kinds. What we make of it, in a search for (true?) Christianity, will no doubt depend upon our norm. Certainly, no churchman would claim that the Church, in the sense of the official, organised institution, has a monopoly of Christianity. The *consensus fidelium* (as in Islam, and in Hinduism) has long been accepted as the arbiter, even of truths formulated by General Councils. Likewise, no Christian would suggest that the Spirit of God is limited to human consciousness, let alone to the rationalistic self-consciousness of the contemporary, individuated bourgeoisie. 'I turn to Christ' is beautiful in its simplicity, and may be a goal of some kind: but the Christian God works also through the influence of stars.

Admittedly, two thousand years are but the twinkling of an eye, in comparison with the hundred thousand generations of man's past. But it should occasion no surprise to any believer in Christ's lordship over the powers that dominate the universe, to discover that, often in silence and sometimes with pain, in this relatively short period he has already achieved fundamental changes in human culture, from within. Indeed, the same may also be said of the Buddha and Mohammed.

Religion changes, as human consciousness changes. As post-industrial society becomes both more cultural and more psychological, and less sociological, in emphasis, so on the one hand the organised and public, and on the other hand the spiritual and private, aspects of the Church become more significant. At the same time, the active Church members become even more important, but as Religious Orders within Christianity. Whereas baptism is enrolment within the supporters of 'Christianity', to be confirmed is to volunteer for this specialised function.

It is both short-sighted, and faithless, for the organised Church to castigate 'Christianity'. Paul might have said, 'To Christ you appeal: to Christ you shall go'. Sometimes the scribes and pharisees, though closest to the Gospel, can be blinded by it. By all means, let the Church challenge 'Christianity'. Yet it must be in love, for there is no profit in adding to the number of ravening wolves. We earn the right to be heard as we remain willing to 'offer it up'.

SEARCHING FOR A FUTURE

DONALD REEVES

Donald Reeves has been Rector of St James's, Piccadilly since 1980. He was ordained an Anglican priest twenty years ago and has worked in parishes throughout the South East. At St James' he has moulded a church which interacts with the community in London's West End on many levels, running lunchtime political debates, psychotherapeutic healing groups, spiritual workshops and a host of cultural activities.

He is an outspoken liberal and radical who is hostile to convervatism whether it is the politics of Margaret Thatcher, the morality of Mary Whitehouse or the theology of Billy Graham.

Radical Christianity

When I was welcomed into the Officers' Mess of the Royal Sussex Regiment, where I served as a National Service Second Lieutenant, I was taken aside by an elderly Major who warned me that there were three topics of conversation banned in the Mess at all times: politics, religion and sex. I could understand the ban on politics: we were all middle class and as army officers thought of ourselves as 'apolitical', another way of saying we were sleeping members of the Conservative Party. I welcomed the ban on talking about sex. There was plenty of that in my platoon and to the ears of an inexperienced nineteen-year-old straight out of an exclusive public school background, very repetitive and strange I found it. But the ban on religion I could not understand. After all, who wanted to talk about religion? It was a most embarrassing topic. I could not imagine any of us wanting to settle down for an evening's chat on the evidence for God, the person of Jesus Christ or the authority of the bible.

My army experience reminded me just how much we like to let our religious beliefs lie quiet and undisturbed. Religion is the parson's job, so the argument goes. He is the one paid to talk about these matters and if he finds he is regarded as an oddball or a harmless fellow that is only to be expected, given our embarrassment about the subject. Even in churches there is the same embarrassment: congregations are much more at ease gossiping about their vicar or each other than about the date of the Exodus. There are, of course, exceptions. A combination of relentless cheerfulness and simplistic certainties found in some churches fascinates, amazes and horrifies those outside the charmed circle of institutional religion (and to some of us inside as well).

However, we are not just a nation of lazy agnostics or cool rationalists. There are many who have jettisoned the dogma but cherish the music or admire the buildings inspired by faith: 'church-crawling' is a hobby not restricted to churchgoers. There are many who have a sneaking admiration for Mother Teresa. There are those too who stroll down memory lane searching for the 'good old days' when the churches were full and upheld the much-vaunted Victorian values. And it is impossible to ignore the persistence of religious attitudes in the popularity of astrology, fortune-telling and some forms of spiritualism (breakfast television has its resident astrologer, but no 'God' spot). Popular religion has a most unsophisticated and readily accessible fatalistic view of our predicament and offers a modicum of consolation and reassurance. Then there are those polls about God. According to them, God is still in business; most of us believe in God. But the polls tell us nothing. They say nothing about the nature of that belief and most of us faced with direct questions about belief in God would probably answer, 'Yes' – just in case.

But together all these indications of the persistence of religious attitudes and practices pale before our embarrassment about religion, and before what may be a new phenomenon in our society which the Churches have hardly begun to address – that is, the presence of religious indifference. This is the most radical form of atheism; even the philosopher Nietzche suffered acutely within himself because of his atheism. But indifference to religion is characterised by a lack of any curiosity about God, or questions about meaning and purpose – for the indifferent, God is dead, and that does not matter. Questions about God have been filed away. I have absolutely no interest in watching international snooker on television; however much others may be captivated, it leaves me cold. I am indifferent to it. Thus it is with questions about religion, about God, about the Churches. For some instead there is the absence of hope; there is resignation, fatalism and despair. For others modest satisfaction is got from doing well whatever it is they do or are driven to do.

I have said that religious indifference is a new phenomenon. But it may well be that the English have always been a sceptical, pragmatic people. Religion may have been truly practised only by a few, even in mediaeval England, and often used politically to 'keep the people quiet' – the rich man in his castle, the poor man at his gate – with the hope of heaven for the poor beyond death. In this case, the decline in numbers and influence of the major Christian denominations is not terminal but characteristic. It may even be, however strange it may seem, that our society is fundamentally based on Christian principles, so it is not important that the Churches are weak or that the attitudes of Christians are not so different from anyone else.

Whatever the historical roots of religious indifference and our embarrassment about religion, its practice is regarded as personal and private – like a hobby. As I write this essay, there is much debate about trading on Sundays. Those in favour of Sunday shopping see it entirely in terms of choice: if people want to go shopping on Sunday, they should. If they want to wash the car, walk the dog, read the Sunday papers, go to church, stay in bed – they should. Looked at in this light, religion is just another commodity to be consumed, mostly by the middle classes. No doubt among the 'disgusted, Tunbridge Wells' brigade who once saw the established Church as an ally in providing security and stability, the sooner the Church of England is privatised the better. But the debate about Sunday trading is only a small, contemporary example of the shrinking of the practice of religion to a personal and private activity, so that church-going is regarded on the same level as playing golf or washing the car or belonging to Rotary. No one objects to a bishop making the most general statements about issues, putting every side of the question, but effectively saying nothing. But once he speaks about a particular issue, he is regarded as meddling in matters which are not to do with him. He is told by his detractors in church and in society to stop interfering; to shut up and attend to the spiritual needs of his people, although these needs are rarely spelt out. The vehemence of those who protest about him speaking out indicates how deep and widespread is the opinion that religion should keep itself to itself. No wonder, they say, our churches are so empty when the Bishops and clergy neglect their spiritual duties.

But the 'privatising' of religion is not new. It is the response of the Churches, particularly the Church of England and the Protestant Churches, to an historical and philosophical process centred round the Enlightenment with roots which can be traced back to the Reformation and beyond.

The shrinking of religion to the personal and private areas of experience was the response to a sustained but often unwitting critique and attack on institutional religion. Faced with the challenge of the Enlightenment, the Churches effectively caved in; the telling of that story takes us far beyond the scope of this essay. All that can be done here is to describe simply some of the invariably unspoken, deeply-felt assumptions about how we understood and explained our experience, at least until very recently.

We believed we had the destiny of the world in our own hands and that through the method of science we could manipulate and control nature. All we had to do was to discover how things work, and then manage them – for our own purposes. These convictions have been accompanied by a sense of a future bright with progress, that happiness was the right of every person and that the nation state has been there to protect that right and create the conditions under which this right could blossom. Such assumptions have provided the rationale for political systems of the right and left; they have lead to the belief that science and technology could, of themselves, provide the prosperity which is our right. Such are some of the fundamental assumptions of Western scientific materialism.

These assumptions are now under question; those ways of explaining our experience are just not adequate. In the last twenty years, there has begun to grow a sense that our civilisation as we know it is coming to an end. The prospect for our future is bleak; the New Jerusalem promised by the philosophers of the Enlightenment has not arrived. Just about all the issues before us seem incapable of any solution: the nuclear threat, a divided world of the North and South, the decay of our cities in the West and the growth of enormous cities in the Third World, the sight of terrorism and violence on our television screen, the rape of the environment and wasteful use of diminishing resources – this familiar catalogue is a grim reminder that our existing institutions cannot cope with these problems, and more seriously, the will to do anything about them collectively is lacking. As the playwright

Samuel Beckett said, "We live between a death and a difficult birth".

Such a time means that, individually and as societies, we are faced with stark choices to carry on as far as possible as usual, which is the natural response of those with power; or to seize the opportunity of a crisis (for that is what I am trying to describe), not so much as a breakdown but as a breakthrough. In Britian, this sense of decay and disintegration has been met by a strongly ideological right-wing Government whose programme sacrifices everything in the interest of the isolated individual, encouraging the Little England attitudes which flourished during the Falklands War. Since 1979 there has been a steady growth of anti-libertarian and authoritarian policies increasingly focused upon law and order. The poor and the black have now become the scapegoats for our problems. If the rich are rich because they deserve to be, the implication is that it is only logical that the poor are poor because they deserve to be and therefore they need to be degraded and humiliated – thus the unemployed and the young blacks, are labelled as the criminal, violent elements responsible for all our ills.

It is a sad comment on our theologians and Christian intellectuals that there has been little or no comment on the collapse of our culture. On the other hand, the reaction to Conservative ideology has been more varied, some of it depressing, some encouraging. It has strengthened the voice of those who see Christian faith as being about the salvation of the individual soul and the Christian life as a preparation of the soul for life beyond the grave. But on numerous occasions the Church has spoken out against evil, and Conservative politicians have been irritated by many statements and reports on poverty, peace, racism, the Third World, the Welfare State. It's a long list. When the history of the Church is written, the Falkland Islands Service in St Paul's Cathedral will probably be seen as a turning point in the relationship between the Churches and the State – where all the major Churches, perhaps conscious of their minority position with little or nothing to lose, planned a service of homage for the sacrifice of our troops who died and mourning for the dead on both sides, rather than a service of thanksgiving which the Government expected.

But if the shape and identity of our Churches is not so recognisable, what then should they become, given the grim realities of our society and the collapse of the old order? We have to insist that the gospel we proclaim is always personal, but that it is never private; or to put it another way, that we have to reverse the habits and practices of nearly 300 years and restore our faith in God to every aspect of experience – personal, yes, but also to everything else, the political, social, economic, and environmental. The Kingdom of God of which Jesus spoke is about the transformation of the whole of creation – never to be realised in this life, but to be fashioned here and there. The Churches have the keys of the Kingdom – so in every place Christians have the awesome responsibility of opening those doors, mediating and celebrating that Kingdom. But this reversal and restoration of faith as central to all human activity depends initially on an urgent and massive spiritual and intellectual effort by theologians, Christian writers, artists, poets and intellectuals to help us recover a way of 'knowing' which is so different from that which wants to order, control and manipulate. It is, to put it in a sentence, about giving the utmost attention to what is there. That means looking evil in the eye and discovering, in the suffering and the disturbances in our society, the call of man to work with God in the liberation of people and the struggle to bring about justice and offer, not pie in the sky when you die, but some hope and reason for living now. Because the times are grave, the issues of defence and poverty, racism and employment are as much moral as political, reflecting ideas about the sort of society we should be creating and the sort of views we hold about the nature of men and women. R. H. Tawney said of the Church of England, "The Church has ceased to count because the Church has ceased to think". That thinking now needs to be undertaken with as much urgency as those engaged in research to stop the killer disease Aids. It is urgent at every level because what is struggling to be born is the beginning of a new Reformation as significant as the Reformation of the sixteenth century. Reformations tell of the closeness of God; thus it is at the philosophical level we need to reconsider how we know anything, and how our ways of knowing God in faith and trust, fragile as they are, are central to the totality of our experience. At another level, it is about restoring the imaginative and intuitive parts of ourselves. At yet another level, there is an urgent task to be done in helping one another to make connections between the Gospel and the historical realities of our lives.

How does this work in practice? It is not clear. The Churches are divided and weak and uncertain. The future is more uncertain and, ultimately, the future is not in our hands. There are no blueprints. It is probable that we are entering another period of the Dark Ages when the old order will collapse and there will be few enough landmarks in the wilderness to find our way around. To some degree all of us are plagued by paranoia about our enemies and succumb to such a sense of fatalism and powerlessness that we can do nothing. But if there is to be a breakthrough, then is it possible to outline some of the characteristics of a genuinely reformed and renewed Christian movement?

To write of a sense or knowledge of the closeness of God just like that is easy enough. To convey this compelling, strange, mysterious knowledge is quite another thing. For an individual or Christian community to have a sense of being 'addressed' or 'called' invites repentance. And it is typical of our tamed, reduced notion of repentance that it is understood as just a matter of saying sorry or giving up some bad habits. It is even more characteristic that we have little idea what a repentant Church would look like. Repentance means turning and letting God be God in us, and recognising God in creation; repentant Churches are sensitive to injustice, free to be joyful and not to take themselves too seriously, and recognise that their security lies with God. A repentant Church is disreputable in the eyes of the world because it is not primarily concerned with its own maintenance or orthodoxy, success or material possessions.

Priorities are easily established. One of them is the unmasking of idols. Our sanctuaries have been stuffed with idols for so long that it has been difficult to see what the living God requires of us. Idols are created by our own hands. We then set them apart, and placate them with expensive gifts. Idols rob us of our power. They turn us into hopeless and powerless people. They tyrannise us; we become dependent on them. A repentant Church becomes conscious of its idolatry, unmasks the idols and reveals them for what they are. Idolatry happens when perfectly reasonable goals like the defence and security of our country, or the expectation of a continually rising standard of living become the 'be all and end all' – ideologies where the means justify the ends, and everything is subservient to those ends. That is why the politics of conviction are so dangerous, when politicians think they and only they are absolutely right and have the truth. But God is truly righteous and is the truth and our convictions are judged by God. The monster in the book of Revelation, representing more than just Imperial Rome, is a terrifying symbol of unbridled power, infecting every part of creation, yet having within it the sources of its own destruction. A penitent Church, conscious of the closeness of God, listening to God's call, discovering the nature of that call through the bible and the history of the Church when it has been most Christ-like, will be cleansed and purified. It will find itself distinctly at odds with the world where the old idols still reign. Our problem has been that, as our practice of religion has shrunk to a private and personal transaction between the individual and God, so we have frequently engaged in idol worship. Our practice of idolatry has turned many of us into crypto-atheists worshipping a tiny god, made absolutely in our own image. But that god is dead. It disables us who worship it. And a Church which worships such a god is not worth saving.

The shape of a reformed Church becomes clearer: it is odd. It does not fit in easily. It is a disturbing influence. Its members are found in all the major denominations; they become aware of the compromises and contradictions of their own institutions. They urge them to practise what they preach, are free to be self-critical, and practise a rigorous process of self-discernment and self-criticism. Thus, for example, they become only too aware that generally the Churches have supported the rich and powerful in the maintenance of their own position and power and have ignored the political demands of the poor.

There is nothing particularly new in all this. Certainly there is no striving after being trendy or relevant. Who wants to suffer for being relevant? As a reformed and penitent Church comes to life so there grows a sense of coming home or of returning to the roots. That is radical Christianity – but it is not an obscurantist, reactionary type of radicalism which offers some sort of private faith untouched by the world. The sense of return is mediated continually, consciously and consistently in our attempt to understand and interpret our experience – personal, yes, but never ever private. Radical Christianity is in the business of making connections.

One of the reasons why 'going to church' and being 'a member of a church' is often so uninteresting is that those connections are never made, and the need to make them is not even recognised. Sometimes serious damage is done, because there is such a longing to make the words and images 'work', that when nothing happens, the Church loses just those who seriously want to undertake a religious journey. But as these connections begin to be made and remade, boredom is dispelled and the will to work for the Kingdom of God in a time of much turbulence is born. No task is more exhilarating, more demanding or more hopeful.

ANDREW WALKER

Andrew Walker is a member of the Russian Orthodox Church and the director of the C.S. Lewis Centre, which studies the relationship between religion and modernity. He teaches philosophy and sociology and is currently honorary fellow of Christian doctrine at King's College, London.

He is a harsh critic of liberal theologians and Bishops who, he believes, have virtually abandoned the essence of the Christian faith, and he argues that all those opposed to liberalism – Eastern Orthodox followers, evangelical Protestants and Roman Catholics – must now bury their differences and unite to save the historic faith of the Christian Fathers.

The Third Schism:

The Great Divide In Christianity Today

When I was asked to contribute an article to "In Search Of Christianity", two images or metaphors came to mind. Firstly, I pictured an expedition organised by the Royal Geographical Society desperately seeking to find the remnants of a fast-disappearing species. No doubt some modern-day Stanley, having been misdirected to the G.L.C.'s Mr. Livingstone, would press on into darkest Hertfordshire in hope (this time) of a genuine sighting of the rare genus *homo christianus*.

But whilst such an image is not entirely idle – in the face of the reality that less than 10% of the British population attend church – I found it soon superceded by a second picture. This time what came to mind was not an adventure nor quest but a search for a good bargain.

Christianity is now on sale in multiform shapes and sizes. Competing in the open market with other religions, there is a bewildering yet broad choice of 'real' and 'best' Christianities for anyone who wants to buy. No doubt someone will soon publish "The Consumer Guide To God" so that people can pop in and out of churches with the same ease and comfort as they visit their favourite restaurants.

'You pays your money and takes your choice' surely exemplifies the 'spirit of the age'; for in our culture religion is not seen as the *raison d'être* of our society and life: it is a series of options which we choose – or goods that we buy – if we feel so inclined. This plurality of religious belief and practice is often applauded as evidence of cultural maturity and tolerance. Nobody forces a version on us any more. There are many varieties on sale vying for our attention, but we, the consumers, have the absolute power of either buying one version in preference to another or withholding payment altogether.

This present collection of essays is itself a demonstration of consumer religion: you (the broad reading public) are being offered a variety of 'goodies' (perspectives) on Christianity. And we (the authors) are selling you our 'lines' like so many religious pedlars in the market place. (Like the BBC's "Thought For The Day" you are being offered, not the Gospel, but the gospel according to the Reverend So-And-So, the personal views of Ms. Suburbia, and the subjective impressions of Dr X).

In this sense, of course, I have to admit to being one of the crowd like everybody else. Whilst I accept the inevitability of this, and whilst I run the logical risk of being hoist by my own petard, I want to assert in this paper that the Christian gospel has a central core of truth that has an objective character about it. To put it in aphoristic form: Christianity is not this or that, but it can be said to be this and not that.

The purpose of this assertion, however, is not so that I can demonstrate this objectivity in a logical way, but in order that I can make out a case that the Christianity of the historic Church, of the ancient creeds and sacred scriptural canons is in danger of being swallowed by something else in the name of religious progress.

To say this is to come clean and admit two things. First, that I am a traditionalist or primitive of sorts, and believe that the Christian faith is founded on biblical revelations concerning a loving God and his incarnation in the world through the historical person of Jesus Christ. Such a belief takes some swallowing today, or in any age, and cannot be demonstrated as factual in a scientific or empirical way. This is not to say, however, that such a belief is false, and certainly it is not to say that it is irrational.

The second thing to admit is that I am not approaching this paper from an Empyrean vantage point nor with the logical disinterest of a mathematical calculator. Christianity, the religion of the apostles, now tattered and divided by schism and heresy – but still bearing the marks of God's grace – has entered the most serious crisis of its two-thousand-year history. I passionately want to see that faith both survive and strengthen in the face of modern Christian alternatives.

I have chosen, therefore, polemic rather than a careful

historical analysis as the medium to express both passion and conviction. The polemic – that Christendom has entered its third and most serious schism – is, I believe, true, and is based on historical argument that is rational and open to refutation. As to whether the schism is a good or a bad thing, that depends on which side of the present divide you stand.

To say that we have entered a crisis in Christendom, which can be characterised as a third schism, necessitates a brief mention of the first two divides, and something about the meaning of schism. Schism is a word that we usually associate with a breach in the unity of the visible Church. The so-called Great Western Schism of 1378–1417, for example, was a break in the unity of the (Western) Catholic Church due to disputed elections to the papacy in which, until the schism was healed, there were competing Popes.

As serious a schism as this was, however, it was not of the magnitude of the really great divides of Christendom. Furthermore, the word schism means to divide, cleave or rend. It is this sense of major division with which I am concerned rather than the idea of a visible split. The first two great schisms of Christianity, between the Eastern and Western Churches, and the Western Reformation, were indeed visible divides. The third schism, because it cuts across denominations rather than between them, is not invisible (we can see it happening), but it is not yet denomination against denomination creating visible and separate camps within Christendom.

The first schism: the divide between the Western and Eastern Churches

It says a great deal for our parochial world-view that Christianity is seen as a Western religion. British students of theology take some time to adjust to the fact that the Western Reformation is only part of a far more fundamental divide of the Christian Church. This division has its origins in the inability of the Greek East and Latin West to cohere.

Although the official date of the Great Schism is 1054, in reality the two halves of Christendom had been pulling apart for centuries. The addition by the Latin West of the word *filioque* ('and the son') to the Nicene creed, which now said of the Holy Spirit 'who proceedeth from the Father *and the son*', and the decision by the Roman See that the Bishop there was to be seen no longer as *primus inter pares* but as possessing superior and unique authority in the Christian Church, are the main reasons cited by Eastern Catholics (the Orthodox) for the Great Schism.

This is not untrue, but it is also the case that the nature of spirituality, liturgy, and theology increasingly developed along separate lines as Eastern and Western cultures evolved and diverged.

Henceforth the Orthodox continued without Pope and without reformation (to this day), and the Catholic Church – cut off from the collegiality of the Eastern sister Churches – went it alone in an increasingly centralised and westernised way. The essential tragedy of the schism was that the universal catholicity of the 'one undivided Church' was broken.

The second schism: the Reformation

The second great divide in Christendom shares with the first schism the characteristic of a gradual breaking down of catholicity. Whilst it may be true that the Roman Catholic Church maintained a powerful hegemony throughout the early Middle Ages, its influence began to wane as Renaissance humanism, the emergence of a natural philosophy that owed little to revelation, and the rise of an embryonic capitalism, weakened the omnipresent authority of the Church. The fact that Martin Luther nailed his famous principles of the Reformed faith to the door of the church at Wittenburg in 1517 is only an historical landmark in the greater reformation of medieval society.

Protestants like to see the Reformation as a great recovery: a return to New Testament Christianity. Undeniably, Protestantism has shown itself to be full of life and vigour, but it has also demonstrated that by its very nature it is schismatic. The Reformation became reformation *ad nauseum:* and modern denominationalism was born.

This was inevitable while the reformers saw Protestantism

as replacing the authority of the Pope by the authority of the bible. It was also the case that now every person was a "pope" who could – and did – interpret the bible according to his own lights.

Furthermore, religious Protestantism paved the way for its own demise and the third schism of recent years. Once it was accepted that scripture stood alone outside tradition, and could be interpreted correctly by anyone with a pure heart and God-given rationality, it was not too big a step to suggest that the same could be said of nature. The emergence of reasoning independent from the Church, begun in the Renaissance, was accelerated under Protestantism, and heralded both the rise of the scientific method and the birth of the philosophical Enlightenment of the eighteenth century.

With the first Great Schism, the West separated from the East; the second schism, the Reformation, saw Protestantism freeing itself from the authority of the Church. The Enlightenment, like Prometheus unbound, tore Western culture away from the authority of the bible. This not only marked the beginning of modern secularism, but it also began the slow process of the third schism.

Since that time, Protestantism has become increasingly naked and vulnerable, as its progeny (the secular doctrines of the Enlightenment) has turned on its parent with all the fury of its Oedipal rage.

The third schism

Christianity in the Third World, and in Eastern Europe, is clearly both growing, and growing in a more orthodox fashion than in Western Europe and North America. It is the West where what I call the third schism has become endemic. As institutional religion has been in decline for one hundred and fifty years, and religious categories of thought have been under constant attack for the same period, this is not very surprising. It is impossible, living in the Western world, not to be influenced by the modern world-view, and the môres and habits of the secular culture.

In the last twenty years since the publication of John Robinson's "Honest To God", the endemic nature of the third schism has become acute; so that today we find that a significant number of ecclesiastical leaders, theologians, and many ordinary men and women, can no longer relate to the central tenets of Christianity as traditionally understood. That is to say that growing numbers (perhaps already the majority) of people want to remain Christian in some way, despite the fact that they can no longer assent to many of the doctrines of the creeds, believe in the bible as a reliable record of historical narratives which includes the virgin birth and resurrection of Christ, or find credible the possibility of miracles in either the past or the present.

Despite the first two great schisms of Christianity, there was enough common ground to assert that there was a family resemblance of Christians, even though the family was separated and relationships impaired. This resemblance was related to a certain 'orthopraxis' – a way of living and behaving that was seen as being connected in some way with an orthodoxy, a right faith or right believing. In practice the link between these two has always been tentative. It cannot be said with certainty that ordinary Christians with little theological training have always grasped the nuances, paradoxes, and presuppositions of the theologians and doctors of the Church. Indeed it would probably be more accurate to assert that orthodoxy, insofar as it existed, was learned more through the medium of liturgy and rite than through sermons or formal treatise. It is an interesting point, for example, that the Eastern Orthodox often translate orthodoxy not as true beliefs, but true worship.

Nevertheless, however true it may be that behaviour and worship tell us more of the nature of Christianity than do its beliefs taken in isolation from practice, it has always been the case that the Christian faith (far more than Islam or Judaism) has been predicated upon certain beliefs which have been held to be true. Michael Goulder, now an atheist who has resigned from holy orders, makes this telling point against his friend John Hick, who remains a 'Christian' yet without believing in either a Holy Trinity or a personal God.

To put the word Christian in inverted commas in this way is not in order to say something unpleasant about John Hick, but in order to register a certain uncomfortableness about the use of the word Christian when applied in this way. I recall a similar lack of ease when Professor Ayer took issue with Don Cupitt's rather cavalier use of the word God in a discussion following the BBC television series, "Sea of Faith". God is not a word to be used in any way we please; it has a meaning that has been sanctioned by usage. Indeed, traditional Christians would want to say that it has a content – a being-in-itself.

Or again, when the Bishop of Durham says that he does not believe in a literal physical resurrection of Jesus from the dead, but thinks that we should understand and believe resurrection in some (unspecified) other way, what does he mean? Is his way of seeing, which is clearly not the way of orthodoxy, a different perception of the same event? A mere question of semantic differences? Or is it a different gospel?

It would be absurd for a member of the Communist Party to declare to his comrades that he no longer accepted the basic tenets of Marxist-Leninism but that he would stay in the Party. It would be simply odd for a Tory member of Parliament to stay in office having publicly renounced free enterprise altogether. At the very least we would want to insist that, if a woman tells us that she is a radical feminist and yet believes in the desirability of patriarchy, her position is inconsistent and logically untenable. We may, of course, think that she is just plain daft like the man who proclaims that he is Napoleon when we know that his name is John Smith.

And yet we find these not unreasonable common-sense observations are so often not applied to Christianity. This may be in part because Christians, these days, are wary of intolerance and bigotry. Heretic-hunting is unfashionable, and certainty and truth are subservient words to authenticity and lovingness. It may be that the strange language of many modern Christians who seem unable to feel at home with the old language (but do they believe in the same realities to which that language pointed?), is itself strong evidence that a major shift in consciousness has occurred. Perhaps, though I use this only analagously, we are witnessing a paradigm shift – a major change in world-view – from the old theological universe to a new one; rather like Newton's cosmology radically shifted to the new scientific world-view of Einstein.

I think that we are undergoing a revolution in thinking and perception which, far from being really new, is in fact the eventual triumph of Enlightenment consciousness over orthodox Christian thinking and experience – in practice, simply, a capitulation to the forces of rationalism and subjectivism. These forces have ushered in a Christianity entirely at odds with Christian tradition.

At times it seems that to stand on the modernist side of the divide is to see oneself as the progressive, the reformer; and the orthodox side as the counter-revolutionary, or, more appositely, the counter-reformer.

From the orthodox side of the third schism, the new Christianity (but not the Christians who make up this new constituency), is the enemy. To stand against it is not reactionary conservativism; it is the stance of the resistance fighter.

Battle lines are by no means firmly drawn, not least because many orthodox Christians are still busy fighting the divisions of the first two schisms. Many of them do not seem to know where the new, and crucial, barricades are. I shall return to this theme in my conclusion. But now I want to outline briefly how the Enlightenment and its consequences brought about the third schism.

The philosophical Enlightenment of the eighteenth century was the dawn of modern optimism, idealism, and intellectual illumination. It was the morning star of modernity without which modern democracy and republicanism would not have been born, and scientific and technological progress would not have been possible. And yet, paradoxically, the Enlightenment had its darker side: the morning star in biblical imagery is, after all, another name for Lucifer.

And yet, Protestants, as if suffering from an incurable 'death wish' have not only attempted to make peace with the darkling child (their offspring) but have grasped him to their bosoms with joy. 'Perhaps,' they have said, 'he may destroy the old religious order, but he will bring new life and make Christianity more authentic, and set it – and society – free.'

But perhaps the new progeny of Protestant society had no

natural filial relationship to Christianity. The child of hope seemed angelic but was in fact a changeling: an incubus whose purpose was to draw out the life blood of its progenitor until it was dead.

We have all seen enough horror movies to know that the vampire first sucks the blood of his victim whilst she is beguiled or sleeping. After a gradual weakening and loss of blood – with only a few tell-tale marks to show what is really happening – the entranced somnabulist, with her life-blood literally draining away, offers her jugular in a final abandonment to her demon lover. She then joins him, keeping the semblance of her former life, but in reality living (if we can call it living) the life of the undead.

Modern Western Christianity may not be undead yet! But a near-fatal incision began with the Enlightenment. From the eighteenth century onwards the world of the senses takes precedence over not only the supernatural world, but also the world of ideas. Newton's great synthesis of natural sciences and cosmology made allowance for a creator, but this God, having made the universe as a clockmaker constructs a clock, withdraws from his creation and leaves it running by its own inviolable laws.

The empirical world, without God, increasingly took the attention. And if there was a tension between the abstract rationality of German philosophers such as Kant and Hegel, and the more pragmatic and empiricist French and British thinkers, there was a common commitment to the primacy of self-knowledge. In Pope's words:

"Know then thyself, presume not God to scan,
The proper study of mankind is man."

As eternal verities were translated into rationalistic philosophy, and miracles were interpreted in the light of the new physics, orthodox doctrines of Christ's divinity and the conundrum of the Holy Trinity came under attack.

Capitalistic economic theory, utilitarianism (that old pagan hedonism in disguise), Kant's progressivism (not to mention Hegel's), and the material and phenomenal world outlook of the philosophers became embodied in the social, economic, and political structures of nineteenth-century Europe.

Modernity was born, and the ideas of the Enlightenment became the stuff of everyday life. In themselves the doctrines of the eighteenth-century philosophers carried conviction but lacked potency. The massive social upheavals of the nine-teenth century, with the move from the country to the towns, the explosion of cities, the dazzling success of science and technology, and the growth of industrialism and bureaucracy, provided the muscles and sinews that enabled the Enlight-enment to come fully to life: it insinuated itself into the consciousness of Victorian men and women, found its way into the language and syntax of both specialist and mundane speech, and created a new culture.

This is not to say that the nineteenth century was not a religious success in some ways. There was the significant growth and influence of conservative Evangelicalism, the rise of Tractarianism, a new outcrop of enthusiastic sectarianism, and a gradual increase in the significance of Catholicism. But the Christian religion, despite these obvious successes, was beginning to show the early signs of anaemia.

This happened in two ways. Firstly, the Churches and their doctrines came under direct attack. Secondly, as the century progressed, many of the Churches internalised more and more of the modern scientific world-view and the method-ology of science itself. Darwinism, and the direct assault on the authority of the Genesis account of creation and *inter alia* the whole authority of scripture is well known. But in fact the doctrines of positivism and science espoused by Auguste Comte since the 1830s, had already declared that both religion and metaphysics were the enemy of progress and reason.

Victorians, including the young John Stuart Mill, were so overcome by the success of the physical sciences, that many believed with Comte that it was only a matter of time before morality and religion would be explained by science. This optimism gave rise to scientism: a doctrine that insisted that all reality and truth were now circumscribed by science. Indeed, for Comte, the young Mill, Spencer, and to a certain extent the mature Karl Marx, science took on the character of true knowledge, whilst religion was reduced to mere opinion.

I think that C.S. Lewis was right when he asserted that Darwinism provided the scientific underpinning for the progressive idealism of Kant's rationality. Once it was believed that progress had a scientific basis, this spilled over into another ideology: the neo-Darwinism that no longer saw itself as a biological theorem but as a principle of progress in the universe itself. This neo-Darwinism is found in Marx, Spencer, and Fabianism, and was later to spawn twentieth-century Fascism.

If the incestuous vampire of Protestantism took time off from his relentless meal throughout the nineteenth century, it was to whisper 'progress, progress' into the ear (so close to the neck) of his victim. 'There will be no apocalypse,' he breathed: 'no Archangel to sound the last trump; heaven is to be built on earth, and the Kingdom of God is to become the kingdom of man.'

Towards the end of the nineteenth century there was a Romantic backlash against the certainties of positivism and scientism. Protestantism partly embraced positivism, and partly tried to disengage itself. Two theological thinkers – and trends – stand out as markers towards the third schism.

Right at the beginning of the century, Schleiermacher, 'the father of modern theology', convinced that Kant had proved the impossibility of approaching God through rationalistic philosophy, and anxious to avoid both sterile rationalism and dogmatic revelation, opted for experience as the touchstone of certainty in faith.

Schleiermacher's influence on Protestant theology has been colossal, and is directly linked with sophisticated and ingenious interpretations of scripture. His experiential theology is not essentially tied to the dogmatics of revelation, and the Jesus experienced in faith is not necessarily the Christ of scripture. Schleiermacher and his many followers today – not least the sociologist Peter Berger – want to resist rationalism and scientism. Berger thinks that experientialism is an antidote to modernism. He must also face the fact that it may be a capitulation to subjectivism.

The emphasis on authentic faith, and careful interpretative

understanding of scripture, was added to in a more scientific way by the Ritschl school of liberal theology in the last quarter of the nineteenth century. Here we see the beginnings of modern criticism so dominant in university departments today. The German scholars began to look at the scriptures not as sacred canon, but as scientific object. They felt that they wanted to go beyond the overlay of theological understanding imposed on the New Testament to the primary data of the historical Jesus.

But the quest for the historical Jesus led to a wedge being driven between the Christ of faith and the first-century Jew from Palestine. Since that time, modern theology has oscillated between a view of Christ as almost all Spirit, bereft of the human-ness of Jesus, or as a mere historical figure empty of divineness.

More generally, the beginnings of historical and textual criticisms in their many forms turned the theological enterprise away from expounding the dogmatics of revelation, to a scientific or interpretative viewpoint. Henceforth the un-examined presuppositions of modern theology were the acceptance of the primacy of rational understanding. The authority of Church or bible was no longer an axiom from which one starts: it was simply data to be examined critically.

Much could be said of twentieth-century developments. When, in the 1940s and '50s, C.S. Lewis warned against the consequences of Christianity absorbing rationalism and scientism and people smiled at the unlikely success of Bultmann's demythologising programme for freeing the 'real' Jesus from a first-century world-view, few orthodox Christians realised that the demon lover had nearly drained the progenitor dry.

In just the last few years, the pace of change has overtaken us. As Goulder puts it:

"We are driving over the same course as our eighteenth-century forefathers, only at four times the speed."

The tremendous interest in the last few years in political and social issues could be grounds for hope; for it is a poor gospel that has nothing to say about oppression, racism and social evils. Yet so often we find secular gospels with theological dressings. Feminist theology, liberation theology, the theology of peace studies or Christian socialism can become what I call constituency theologies where the social or political concern simply swallows the theology.

But if only Western Christianity – and we are now talking about all of us, not just Protestants – could wake up or be roused before the engorgement of the demon is complete, it would discover a remarkable thing. Whilst it lay sleeping and dreaming dreams of authentic and mature religion (no longer innocent after feeding from the critical tree of knowledge), the incubus that was drawing its life force so steadily yet so sweetly had already turned Enlightenment man into a living corpse.

This is the truth for which the gospel of Jesus Christ and his apostles is literally salvation. Modernity, the Enlightenment's child, has brought material wealth and medical aid in a manner undreamed of two hundred years ago. But it has also brought us to the verge of extinction through nuclear war and ecological folly. The West has hoarded most of the wealth for itself, and divides it in a way which is unjust. Materialism and the reality of the phenomenal world has all but drowned out the still small voice of the heart. At the very moment that systems-analysis in government and micro-chip technology in business and education take us yet further into a rationalistic society, our moral structures are falling apart.

The flip-side of scientism so easily becomes nihilism. At the moment that the certainty of science is praised to the skies, traditional morality and orthodox religion are dismissed as 'mere conventions', 'wish-fulfillment', or 'subjective delusions'. Enlightenment man has undoubtedly been a man of power, but he has also been a barbarian. Now he is stumbling.

The Church should not be helping him up, but helping him over: false optimism does not need a helping hand; it needs firstly the truth, and secondly love to salve the lost illusions and move on to a fuller humanity.

People in the inner cities, the unemployed, those living in fear of annihilation from nuclear war, no longer believe the empty words of progress. But can the new Christianity, the

Christianity that has become so synergistic with the modern world – so infused with the life-force of the incubus – preach a gospel of hope to heal the despair? The short answer is no, not until it exorcises its own demon, and ceases to live its undead existence.

But will the orthodox Christians, scattered and divided by the first two schisms of Christendom, fare any better? Do they have a gospel for a fallen culture? The short answer is that they do, though it is not a new gospel.

The old story needs retelling and reformulating in the idioms of a modern world weaned on the realities of technologies and consumerism. But the truths of the story remain the same. God is love, and it is in the nature of love that it offers itself to others. But others, in order to receive love, must be free to reject it, and free to choose for themselves whether they will return it. Since the creation of the world, people have chosen to reject God and love, and have preferred selfishness and self-knowledge. The old-fashioned word for this is sin. But sin written large in the cultures and nations of our planet has wrought divisiveness, war, and separation.

Although we wonder whether the suffering and evil of existence is too high a price to pay for freedom, God takes the initiative in our agony and confusion, and, divesting himself of his power and glory, enters into solidarity with us in the person of Jesus. We read in the gospels that Jesus healed a leper by touching him and yet did not become leprous himself. Similarly, as God-man, Jesus entered truly into our human condition and yet was not overcome or contaminated by the unlovingness and destructiveness of human evil.

He conquered and redeemed us from within our own humanity, and then finally this man of love was taken "without a city wall" and crucified. Love, however, also conquered death; that final enemy that separates us from each other and destroys hope and joy. The risen Christ returned to God the Father having established a bridgehead between fallen humanity and perfect love, which is God himself. Jesus, having left the world, sent the Holy Spirit – that aspect or 'person' of God's nature that heals and comforts, and pleads – to re-establish communion and

215

unbroken love between God and man. To become a Christian is to become not only a believer and follower of Christ, but to be supernaturally or spiritually joined to him through the enabling power of the Spirit. In that sense the Church is one body of Christ.

Jesus, who is the head of the Church, which is the body, not only shows the way of love and reconciliation. He is the way: the path from our broken and fallen humanity to a new humanity which acquires the stature of Love itself.

The history of salvation is essentially an unfinished love story. It begins simply, in the words of John's gospel, "For God so loved the world . . ." The story never ends because love is limitless. But we are a long way from limitless love, and the modern world with all its mastery of nature and self-knowledge seems incapable of finding it. I do not believe that the new Christianities, predicated as they are upon either rationalism or subjectivism, really believe any more that God is love, nor do they knew how to tell his story.

But orthodox Christians, who can tell God's story in many different ways, and with different though complementary emphases, are not preaching this message with any prophetic power because they are too busy still fighting the first two schisms. It is difficult to convince a fallen culture that there is an ultimate and saving love in the universe when Christians squabble and fight like any other human family. There is no doubt that the message of God's love is simple, perhaps deceptively simple for modern man, but the way of love is unbearably hard.

In order to show that love, and in order to prevent the third schism becoming Christianity's final divide, orthodox Christians will have to come together and put aside their differences (except when conscience absolutely forbids it).

A radical realignment of forces, however, is useless as a pious hope. It needs concrete action. Evangelicals must open themselves to Catholics and Orthodox. The Roman Catholic Church must enter the British Council of Churches (despite the very real risk that this could exacerbate the old second schism and even worsen the third schism). Anglo-Catholics and Evangelicals within the Church of England will have to come out from their separate corners and join hands. The

Church Society must decide whether it is still defending the sixteenth-century Reformation or fighting today's war. West Indian Pentecostals and Greek and Russian Orthodox will have to come out of their ghettos and remember that they are in Britian as missionaries. The Catholic and Protestant Truth Societies will need to form a Christian Truth Society.

All of this, of course, sounds like a sort of madness; certainly a kind of desperation. But believing in love and proclaiming a gospel of hope is not a sort of fatalism that says 'it will all come right in the end'. Paradoxically, love has to be fought for. Christianity is being subverted by the forces of darkness (however reasonable and rational they seem). This calls for warfare. Nothing less.

ELAINE STORKEY

Elaine Storkey is a Christian feminist who teaches philosophy at Oak Hill theological college and is a sociology tutor with the Open University. She has taught women's studies in Britain and the United States and has been involved in counselling women.

She has been a Christian for more than twenty years but has only become a feminist within the past four years, during which she has been speaking, writing and broadcasting on women's issues. Her most recent work is "What's Right with Feminism?".

The Future For Women

It is no secret that the search for Christianity has traditionally been easier for women than men. For though its leaders have almost universally been male, the Christian Church has drawn its strongest grass-roots support from women. There are, of course, many reasons for this. It could be that because of the way women are regarded in society they have had less status and face to lose in admitting their vulnerability and weakness. It could be that having enjoyed greater freedom to express their emotions they find it easier to confess their sins and express their need of a Saviour. Whatever the reason, it is clear that women have formed the powerful back-up services of the Church and ensured that the next generation is acquainted with the Christian gospel.

Today, there are many groups of women set against the Church and attacking the Christian faith from a feminist perspective – and I believe this could have potentially alarming consequences. For if women who have traditionally been so loyal begin to turn their backs on Christianity, then it would indeed present the Church with a grave crisis.

The Church faces a real dilemma. Should it actively encourage women to work through questions of their own identity, sexuality, economic status and social role? Or should it reassert its traditional teaching: that women are subject to men and should be submissive, dependent, domestic and pure? In fact, it is because Christians often continue to maintain the latter against the attack from secular feminists that women in the Church feel increasingly isolated and confused.

This isolation arises because women encounter, deep in their own experiences, a level of discrimination which feminists understand but which fellow Christians cheerfully ignore or even justify with reference to 'Christian values' or 'women's roles'. The confusion and isolation deepens because many feminists are saying that Christianity is intrinsically

X REM. A clear parallel begins to appear between this and the preceding article incapable of understanding women or offering them full affirmation of their personhood. The future for women in Christianity centres on whether this statement is true – and it is this which I want to examine in detail.

At the heart of the feminist attack on Christianity is the notion of patriarchy. Patriarchy, the dominance of men over women, is structured into all social relationships. It is there in marriage, in work, in business, in the professions, in the law, in education. It is there in male violence and sexual abuse. It is strong in the Two-Thirds World as well as in the industrial West. Patriarchy is everywhere: in the White House, the Kremlin, the Politburo, the Broederbond, the Vatican. It is present in our financial empires, our universities, our political parties, our legal structure, our economy, and our Churches. It undergirds all human systems, whether capitalist, Marxist, tribalist, Hindu, Islamic or Christian. Mary Daly, herself a former Catholic theologian turned radical feminist sums up their case: "Patriarchy is the prevailing religion of the entire planet."

The last point is the crucial one. For feminists are saying that Christianity has not resisted patriarchy or challenged the world's way of seeing things. Far from it. It has bowed the knee to patriarchy. It has upheld and reinforced it. It has accepted male dominance wholesale. So although women have supported the Church, the Church has not supported women. Instead it has kept women down, and in doing so has shown that it is fundamentally no different from any other religion or ideological system. Even worse, it actually gives patriarchy the divine seal of approval. If this is true, why has the Christian Church upheld patriarchy so contentedly? As far as feminists are concerned the first reason lies in its view of women. The second lies in its view of God.

Traditional 'Christian' views of women

Many of the Church's attitudes to women have been patronising and derogatory. From the early Church Fathers onwards a sharp distinction has been drawn between women and men, with much of the blame for evil in the world being thrown at women. It is not difficult to see why Tertullian,

Chrysostom, Augustine and Aquinas are all alleged to be misogynists. It is hard indeed for feminists to forgive Tertullian for his heavy-handed treatment of women.

> "You are the devil's gateway. How easily you destroyed man, the image of God. Because of the death which you brought upon us, even the Son of God had to die."

Clement of Alexandria took up the same theme: that women are shameful by nature and the source of sin in man. Augustine is said to argue that only man is made fully in the image of God, and again holds woman responsible for the Fall. To Chrysostom is imputed one of the earliest Christian justifications of the public/private dichotomy, and the forbidding of women ever to venture into the public arena. The disastrous example of Eve hangs over women to eternity:

> "The woman taught once, and ruined all. On this account . . . let her not teach. . . The whole female race transgressed."

This view of women became systematised in Church law by the jurist Gratian:

> "[Man] has the image of the one God. Therefore woman is not made in God's image. Woman's authority is nil; let her in all things be subject to the rule of man . . . Neither can she teach, nor be a witness, nor give a guarantee, nor sit in judgement. [For] Adam was beguiled by Eve, not she by him'.

The views of Thomas Aquinas were also hardly flattering. Combining the attitudes to women from his predecessors along with Aristotelian notions of biology he came up with the conclusion that women were "defective and misbegotten": "for the active force in the male seed tends to the production of a perfect likeness in the masculine sex, while the production of women comes from a defect in the active force." His notion of woman as helpmeet is also seen as derogatory, since he accepts her as a helpmeet only in the process of procreation. In every other respect man is helped better by another man.

Misogyny such as this was thus bound to influence the

developing Church, and indeed continued to do so through-out the Middle Ages. What is more, it also ensured that often pagan attitudes of the day became part of Christian practice. And although views of women improved considerably with the Reformation they did not move far enough. John Knox's now infamous "First Blast of the Trumpet Against the Monstrous Regiment of Women" voiced the feelings of many other men in the Church. At the same time, of course, it was also opposed by others of the reformers as being altogether too excited and demeaning to women. Luther and Calvin certainly moved away from the still-held Catholic belief that women were unclean and agents of the devil. And yet even they did not see them as equal to men. However, surely all his was a long time ago? Why is it still such a sore point for many women? Can't they just let bygones be bygones? The answer from feminists is that these are no bygones. Underneath a more sophisticated veneer and a more liberal theological framework these same attitudes are still held by the Church today. Even though women have won a measure of recognition in the wider society (and this is pitiful enough), responses within the Christian Church still evidence the same assumptions of women's inherent inferiority and the need for their subordination. Stereotypes of women as less rational, more emotional, more vulnerable, domestic and nurturant are still trotted out in an attempt to justify inequalities in pay, in educational and promotion opportunities, and to give lip service to the importance of their task as mothers. (Yet the majority of these mothers find themselves doing two full-time jobs because the myth of a 'family wage' is not an actuality in many homes). These same stereotypes are also effectively used to exclude many women from exercising their talents in the ministry of the Church. We might have learnt how to put it in a more refined way than John Knox, but, apart from our language, little has changed.

The Christian writer Stephen Clark tells us "Male aggressiveness equips men to protect and lead the social groupings. Superior visual-spatial ability may equip men to cope with broad social structural questions ... [This] harmonizes well with an overall governing role. A governor must be able to take disciplinary perspective, to be detached, to order a situation". On the other hand ... "... in every known society women have cared for the young children and managed the domestic sphere. The female family bond certainly equips women for this role, as does female nurturance."

This vision of women as essentially and naturally home-centred and domestic (and thus by implication out of place anywhere else) is so pervasive as to have become an ideology.

In so much Christian writing women are still seen as derived from men and existing for men; they are also still largely required to keep silence in churches. And for many feminists no amount of theological argument can justify the inherent sexism of this position.

Traditional views of God

Feminists claim there is a deeper and more insidious reason for the attitudes the Church has towards women. It lies in its attitude to God. For the view apparently held, and undoubtedly propagated, by people in the Church is that God is male. The Trinity is male. Christ, the male Son of a male Father comes to earth to die for men. Then, of course, the Jewish patriarchs were male, the twelve apostles were male. What is more, argue the feminists, whatever we think of the authority of the bible, there is no avoiding the fact that it was written down by men. And for so many women this is the final statement of the irrelevance of Christianity to them.. The Christian faith proclaims, endorses, and affirms a male-centred universe. The male is norm. In the words of one sympathiser, "If God is seen as simply and exclusively male, then the very cosmos seems sexist".

Mary Daly makes the point another way: "If God is male, then the male is God." If the Church is in the business of worshipping a male God there is no way out of patriarchy. For here in the very focus of our commitment, in the author of all reality, the sustainer and upholder of the universe, the principle of male power is upheld and justified. Inequality for women is structured into creation itself. The male God has established male rule and female subservience. To accept Christianity means accepting this as a fact of life.

This centrality of the male is echoed in all the language, the liturgy and the theology and the worship of the Church. The female is either subsumed and swallowed up in the male, or is ignored altogether. Many books by Christians adopt, even unconsciously, an implicit acceptance of this position. Women are invisible, even in book titles: "The Glory of Man". Hymns, sermons, church services all give out the same message. We sing of "brotherly love", of the "faith of our fathers". The opening call to worship in the Anglican liturgy addresses us as "Dearly beloved brethren." Women do not have to be denied access to leadership positions in order to feel superfluous. Many women tell me that their irrelevance shrieks at them with a hundred different voices.

Disillusionment with the Christian Church and indeed with Christianity as a whole has therefore been articulated by an increasing number of women over the last ten years. The gauntlet is thrown down. Surely it calls for a response?

Refusal and rejection

The most frequent response is refusal to take feminists seriously, simply to ignore and reject their arguments. For what right have women outside the Church, who do not begin to subscribe to a Christian belief system, to raise these kinds of issues? What gives them the authority to tell the Church how it should write its theology and its liturgy or manage its affairs? And this response is a reasonable one. Christianity can only be understood fully from a point of commitment. So one conclusion has been for the Church to close its door to the turmoil on its doorstep. However, the noise has not stayed on the doorstep. For inside the Church women have started to ask the same questions. Not now with the intention of attacking or destroying the faith but of reworking it to rid it of sexism. Groups such as Women in Theology, the Catholic Women's Network, the International Alliance of St Joan, Men Women and God and the Community of Men and Women in the Church, all take seriously the need to look again at traditional views of women, and at the male images of God to see if the Church is doing justice to the Christian faith. Yet all these efforts

225

frequently fall on deaf ears. In so many ways the Church hierarchy in many denominations stays unflinching. Even where arguments are persuasive, caution is always advised. For many feminists this simply means they will continue to be ignored for many more years.

As well as those who ignore, there are, of course, those who attack. Many in the Church sense a deep threat from the feminists, a threat which is both theological and personal. Even among those who try to understand what feminists are saying there is disquiet, alarmism and misrepresentation. After reading William Oddie's "What Will Happen to God?" the average Christian could be forgiven for thinking that all feminism within the church will ultimately lead to goddess worship, apostasy and atheism. It would seem that once 'feminine' imagery for God is taken from the scriptures into worship, we are at once advocating 'revolution and nothing else'. To recognise that the bible also likens God to a mother is interpreted as 'The revolt against God the Father', and as a short step from the annihilation of the Christian faith.

Retreat

This attack, of course, is not totally unfounded. There are undoubtedly women who have gone in this direction. There are women who have begun within the Christian tradition, but have become deeply disenchanted with its sexism, and feel intensely alienated and excluded. These same women have increasingly identified with other women for whom a male God is as irrelevant as a male Santa Claus, and together they have begun to work through and live in a woman-centred alternative. The result is a retreat from the Christian faith. Post-Christian feminism is both a vehement attack on traditional Christianity and an affirmation of female autonomy. The deepest values are those of radical feminism, which sees itself forced to exclude men because to include them always ensures male dominance on any agenda. So such women have begun by trying to accommodate a feminist view of reality, based on an Enlightenment view of human autonomy with a Christian faith-commitment. But a belief in ultimate human independence, be it male or female, is in the

226

end in fundamental opposition to a Christian position. For Christianity says above all that we are creatures, we are sinful, we are essentially dependent on a creator who made us. And so the conflict becomes a total one. For those feminists it can only be resolved by dropping one of their basic articles of faith. If we cannot hold together both the ultimate autonomy of woman and a commitment to the Christian God, then God will have to go. But the exit is not a painless one. For all the hurt and anger, the disappointment and loss at this resolution of the struggle, is thrust upon the departing God and the Church which would enshrine him. Amongst the most vociferous opponents to the Christian faith would therefore be those women who have tried and failed to accommodate their need for affirmation as women with their belief in God.

Rediscovery

Many women and men are increasingly unhappy with either of the two responses outlined so far. Many men actually do not feel content to ignore the issues and attack the feminists. Conversely many Christian feminists are not willing to redo theology in such a way that the gospel loses any distinctiveness. Rather they want to see this distinctiveness operate in its understanding of women. Is there another way forward?

A lot depends on where the main blockages are. It will make a difference if we are able to locate the roots of sexism in Christianity. Do we see it as firmly anchored in scripture itself, or is sexism rooted in the Church's response? Is the bible a male chauvinist document, or has the Church incorporated male chauvinism into its tradition without scriptural approval? A gut response is to say quickly that a more 'authoritarian' approach to the Bible inevitably brings a more authoritarian response to women. Yet is this always the case? Certainly it is by no means true that those who hold firmest to a strong view of bibical authority are inevitably those who stifle the talents of women. It is very often those who have a much looser view of scripture who prop up the male hierarchy most firmly.

The choice then seems to be either to reorganize the

scriptures or to reorganize the Church. I favour the latter. As a teacher of philosophy I am acutely aware how heavy scepticism towards the biblical texts carries with it many sets of often unexamined assumptions. Philosophical pre-suppositions, derived usually from contemporary empiricism, are embedded in the apparently 'objective' and questioning attitudes which are brought to the bible. Interestingly, many philosophers have seen the weaknesses in these positions a decade ago. Theologians are always slower on the uptake.

But there are other reasons than the weaknesses of liberal theology which would make me rely on the scriptures rather than on Church tradition. For what they have to say about God is what many women (and men) have experienced in the depths of their being to be true, even if the Church as a whole has sometimes missed out on it. For it could just be that what many in the Church have been so intent on defending or passing on as the Christian faith has been defective and actually out of step with biblical revelation. The way forward seems then to me to be to rediscover the biblical truth about God, and to recognize that the gospel is 'good news' for women.

Is God male?

Actually no. The problem is that, following the example set in the bible, we inevitably refer to God as 'he' and we pray to 'God our Father'. This gives us the natural feeling that this God must therefore be male. Yet what kind of God is behind the male personal pronoun? It is a God who reveals himself as a person but not as a male. The problem, in fact, is one of language, not of sex. For to be a human person is to be either male or female, so we feel that it must be the same for God. Yet even a brief reflection will show us that if we get closer to a biblical understanding, this will be impossible. For the God who reveals himself as the creator of both male and female cannot simply be either of these. For both men and women are made in the image of God, despite the misunderstandings of the early Church Fathers. (The first chapters of the bible cannot properly be understood in any other way, and thankfully this is now widely acknowledged). Two con-

228

Men *is* simply because God *is* power: sex *is* purely biological distinction difference

clusions follow, either of which is acceptable to feminists searching for God. Either God, as the author of all sexuality, is beyond sexuality in the same way that as the author of time he is beyond temporality. Or God who gives his image to both men and women can therefore be understood and described in both male and female terms. At different times the scriptural texts emphasise each of these positions. We focus so much on the male images of God given in the bible, and there are many. But there are also female images which have so often been downplayed or ignored because the notion of a male God has been prominent in our thinking.

This is the same with our understanding of God the Father. When Christ invites us to call God 'Father' he is not making a point about God's gender, but about the relationship we can have with God. We can call him 'Abba' – Daddy – and have that intimate, gentle and caring relationship which a very young child knows with a parent. Nor again does this exclude God having a motherly relationship with us. Again we have biblical images which liken God to a mother. The crucial point is that God is our parent, both in the sense of being our maker, but also in this new, gentle and very tender way which Jesus Christ opens up for us. For most of us, to pray to our Father God, expresses this wonderfully. But those who cannot accept the exclusive notion of 'Father' because they cannot see it apart from maleness do not have to reject Christianity because of it. The problems arise because we take anthropomorphic images too seriously. The first commandment could help us here. God is bigger by far than our language.

Finding Jesus

A feminist's search for Christianity ends, like everyone else's, when she finds Jesus. But how difficult the Church often makes this for us. Jesus is so often shrouded in male mystery, served up by male Popes and Archbishops with male pomp and circumstance. What a far cry from the Jesus of the gospels. For in that Jesus we see a man who derides hierarchy, who warns his disciples against ambition and wanting to be in positions of prominence. We see Jesus who, though he was God, made himself of no reputation. We see Jesus who was a friend to women, to the poor, the discarded, the rejected; Jesus who washed the dirty feet of his disciples; Jesus who died for people even whilst they were "yet sinners". We see Jesus the servant, and in his service he offers us freedom.

It is when women meet this Jesus that their hearts are warmed, their fears removed, their anger is melted and they know peace with God. For Jesus cut across his culture's stereotyping of women as fools or seductresses. He broke the rigid Jewish taboos which saw women as defiling. Instead he gave them dignity, value and approbation. He was not patronising or scornful. He did not ridicule or dismiss women. Women were among his closest followers. They supported him financially. They identified with him fully.

The quickest glance at Christ's relationships with individual women reinforces all of this. When a woman with a twelve-year long haemorrhage 'defiles' him by touching his cloak and receives healing he does not rebuke her, but commends her faith. He is prepared too to make himself ritually unclean, and disregard the raised eyebrows of his disciples by asking for a drink from a Samaritan women at the well. More than that, with total disregard to her low status as woman and a Samaritan it is to her that he reveals himself as the Messiah. He has no condemnation either for the woman taken in adultery, but prevents her death, telling her to sin no more. He is prepared to accept the love, kisses, tears and affection of a woman who 'shames' herself by letting down her hair and wiping his feet. When this raises a scandal Christ merely turns on the men and asks why they had not been able to show him this love and warmth and practical concern.

It is the woman who listens and learns he commends more than her sister who is busily accepting the Jewish ideology of women. And yet to this sister he also discloses himself as the resurrection and the life. It is the vulnerable woman, the widow, the mother, the daugher, the menstruating, for whom he shows compassion and concern. For Jesus is more than their friend. He is their Saviour, their representative.

Those who stress the maleness of Jesus, then, miss the point entirely. For Jesus did not come as man but as human being. He is indeed the Word-made-flesh, not the word-made-male. His concern to make this clear to women at every opportunity is reflected even in the language he uses in his parables. Not for him the lofty, formal masculine homilies. But he uses images and examples that every woman would understand: grinding corn, yeast and bread, looking for lost coins, sewing new cloth on old garments, persistent widows. Harsh words were never for women. They were for the powerful, male, patriarchal establishment: greedy business-men, Jewish religious leaders, kings and rulers.

Searching for Christianity, then, means searching for Jesus. And when we find him it opens up a whole new vision of life beyond the Church into every area. For Jesus endorses women as women, not only in Christian worship but in every aspect of life in society. When we as women have been there with those early sisters at the foot of the cross, and known, like them, the reality and power of his resurrection then our search is 'over. Christianity is Christ. And Christ is our redeemer, our friend, our joy and our liberator.

TONY COXON

Tony Coxon is Director of the Social Research Unit at University College, Cardiff. He went to train as an Anglican ordinand at Mirfield, where he was the first student to be allowed to read sociology and philosophy. In consequence he renounced his faith and became a sociology lecturer.

After seven years he returned to the Christian faith, but recognised that his vocation was *not* to be a priest. He has co-written "The Fate of the Anglican Clergy" and is currently researching the impact of Aids on gay lifestyles.

Whither the Church?

Every Christian has excellent reasons, should he or she want them, for renouncing the Church. In 1927 H. Richard Niebuhr expressed the basis of these reasons succinctly and well:

> "Christianity has often achieved apparent success by ignoring the precepts of its founder. The Church, as an organisation interested in self-preservation and in the gain of power, has sometimes found the counsel of the cross quite as inexpedient as have national and economic groups . . . it found that it was easier to give to Caesar the things belonging to Caesar if the examination of what might belong to God were not pressed."

It isn't just that the Church (by which I mean the institutional Church throughout) is fallible, or even that the fallibility of its members detracts from its status as redeemed bride of Christ, for in this case organisational penitence or greater individual holiness could solve the problem. And it manifestly does not do so, for the Church has often been most holy in conditions of gross corruption and least holy in eras and areas of highest piety. Perhaps surprisingly, those who remain in the Church can usually produce a more extensive, profound and damning set of reasons for leaving than those who do in fact leave.

If we are to understand this paradox – as we must if we are to interpret aright what is going on in Christianity today – we have to begin by looking *not* at the Church as a theological or supernatural entity but, initially at least, as a natural social institution. Whereas the Christian is prone to exclude everything except God's hand from analysis of the Church, the sociologist is likely to see how far religious organisations can be explained without invoking non-natural intervention. There is no *necessary* incompatibility between these two accounts – after all, God does work through natural and social channels, and it would be a curious theology of incarnation which viewed that as anything but normal. Nonetheless, there is tension – the sociologist often wants to go on to exclude *any* divine operation, and the Christian gets worried by the fact that things felt to be uniquely 'religious' are neither unique to Christianity, nor purely individual in form. For instance, Felicitas Goodman, in her fascinating "Speaking in Tongues" points out the remarkable similarities between a pentecostalist sect in Mexico City, Maya Indians in Yucatan and a white congregation in Indiana. These similarities cover not only linguistic and paralinguistic features, but also the socially structured way in which participants behaved. This remarkable degree of social patterning seems at first sight to be totally incompatible with the highly personalised action of the Spirit, and as the sociologist Martin Marty said in reviewing the book:

> "The thousands who gather at Pentecostal conferences . . . are not likely to make Dr Goodman their patroness. Her findings imply potentially devasting questions for them and their claims."

But equally, as she herself says, observing the phenomenon was awesome in its own right and it can perfectly well be argued that the common features she observed were due to the same Holy Spirit operating. Though rather more pedestrian, the developments in the organised Churches in the past few decades present virtually identical questions of parallel interpretation, and for my part I want to press the sociologists' claims.

This may sound like a clarion-call to scientism – the attempt to elevate the empirical and knowable to privileged status – but it is not. It is a procedure well understood in Roman Catholic circles for testing the miraculous, and it is perhaps a pity that it is not turned on the Church itself in a similar manner. Nor is it a disguised version of a purely Marxist analysis, valuable though that might be as an ingredient of the explanation. For in the last resort an authentic Marxist explanation of religion must be atheistic, and no amount of theological sophistry or metaphysical Marxism can alter that.

Enough of preliminaries. Suppose we now take aboard such sociological explanation and look at contemporary Christianity, what contribution does it make to the diagnosis and prognosis of the condition? The most monumental attempt to describe and explain the tension between the radical claims of the gospel and the conservation of the institutional Churches was that of Ernst Troeltsch, in "The Social Teachings of the Christian Church". There he emphasised the sociological distinction between the Church and the sect. These two categories of Church and sect described what he felt were two quite distinct types of organisation, whichhad distinctive structures, recruitment – and social teaching. These are certainly still identifiable categories, even if more recent developments have made the distinction more hazy. Most importantly, Troeltsch saw that *both* types of structure were present in the early Church, and this insight is crucial if we are to understand what is happening today, for virtually all renewal or revivalist movements in this century have originated *within* a Church.

Pre-eminent among Troeltsch's successors, Richard Niebuhr looked instead at the *process* whereby sects in effect became 'half-way' churches, especially in the United States, and coined the ugly term 'denominationalisation' to describe it. The cyclical process of renewal, schism and institutionalisation well describes certain periods of Christianity, and the succession of Ivy League Universities down the East Coast of the USA testifies to the repeated southwards move of 'purer' puritanism, just as the complexities of Hebridean Presbyterianism represent the detritus of nineteenth-century renewal.

Seeing the sect (whether within or without the Church) as embodying the radical impulses of Christianity is appealing, but there are still problems. The emergence of a small group of highly committed, enthusiastic, proselytic enthusiasts poses obvious threats to all Church structures, not just the more traditional ones, since it questions the form and basis of that authority and challenges it to live up to some understressed or forgotten aspect in a way that is often sociologically impossible for it to do. Time after time it has been money which has been the presenting symptom, seized on by renewal and reform movements, and an established Church structure could not institutionalize what we know of Jesus's approach to money (or for that matter to many other things). So the activities of the Church Commissioners, for instance, can certainly be further restrained within certain bounds, but they could not literally respond to the gospel demand without ceasing to be. The same could be said of peace, authority, sex – Jesus's apparent attitudes and demands seem to be incapable of being institutionalised, nor was he very interested in the possibility of whether they could be.

But the growth of new movements is also inherently self-defeating. Sociological analysts from Max Weber on have stressed that radical sects are inherently unstable, liable to either disintegration or routinisation. Once a movement grows and continues, it immediately hits the problem of succession beyond the founder's life. The second generation cannot be routinely inspired, converted or over-committed, as any parents know to their cost, and forms of education, instruction and rational decision-making inevitably change the nature of the movement and set it irrevocably on the path of institutionalisation, compromising the original pristine values and sowing the seeds of a subsequent renewal.

This paradox is at the heart of any social institution, and simply takes on an acute form in Churches. In the case of Christianity, the resolution has always been an unhappy, none-too-stable compromise. Realists from Constantine to Calvin and from Shaw's inquisitor in "St Joan" to Koestler's commissar have seen this clearly and correctly: the most apparently incompatible structures appear to be necessary to allow the luxury of revolt and renewal to occur and perpetuate the original vision. A sophisticated realist could go on to say that the very tension which this generates makes such structures redeemable, but then so could Josef Stalin, no doubt.

Equally the radicals have usually been unwilling to accept such institutional compromise. St Francis of Assisi is unusual in this respect and provides an illuminating instance. How was the Roman Church of the time to contain such a radical

237

renewal movement, having manifestly failed to contain many similar heresies of the time? In a recent book a member of the Little Brothers of Jesus, deeply committed to St Francis's ideas, has had to make Francis benefit from eight centuries of historical hindsight and maturation in order to resolve the paradox, by having him say:

> "Oh, I would not have proposed this manner of life [poverty] for every one. For example, it would not have been the thing for my father.
>
> *That would have been impossible. Society had other laws. People had different callings.*"

The first paragraph could well have come from *il poverello*; the second comes from a person who has to live with the attempt to make Francis's inspired gesture and an individual commitment into a general principle. The notion of 'calling', important as a way of containing and controlling the call to poverty, was later to produce quite opposite consequences when the monastic calling was taken by the Lutheran entrepreneur to the outside world. Any attempt to contain or to generalise such unequivocal gospel demands – necessary though that may be – is bound to produce unforeseen and often paradoxical consequences. Far from being naive, then, it is the radicals who remain within the institutional structure who are most attuned to the paradoxical nature of the Church as an institutional and as a revolutionary force, and it is the marginal person who combines the security and the comfort of belonging with the excitement and cross-pressure of being at the boundary.

At this point, with the invocation of individual human needs as an integral part of the Church's institutional structure, we may well move to von Hügel's approach to resolving the paradox, which had much in common with that of his friend Troeltsch. Von Hügel also saw the Christian progression as a threefold list: institution, intellectual and mystic, corresponding to the stages and needs of infancy, adolescence and adulthood. The 'institutional' is now explicitly seen as including the type of parental authority so often assumed in papal, episcopal (and, in general, clerical) pronouncements, the 'intellectual' clearly includes the radical and critical component often at the root of renewal and sectarian movements, and the 'mystical' encompasses 'religionless' Christianity as much as the exploration of the inner self. If everyone has components of these three things in his or her makeup, and can be characterised by a profile describing what mixture of these three things predominates, and if the Church responds to this trio of needs, then the problem is to find the organisational structure best fitting the individual needs, and the organisational problem is how to satisfy a set of somewhat incongruous needs within one organisation.

There is a certain plausibility in this idea of a type of selective assortment of people into basically congruent structures, and it also helps us to interpret what is happening around us.

There are other consequences and fictions which need exploring and emphasising within this framework. A most persistent and pervasive one has to do with commitment. Unlike the sect, Churches encompass a far greater range of commitment, from nominal adherence to the fanatic. But important decisions, policy and publicity are made by those at the upper ends of that spectrum of commitment, as many politicians have learned to their cost. It is the faithful attender of ward meetings, the reliable canvasser, the faction newspaper-seller, the well-informed proselytiser who makes the Labour Party leader's life hell, and it is the silent union or party members – with thoughts duly and comfortably articulated by the leadership – who supposedly form the resevoir of sensible moderation when it comes to tempering the radical. So, too, the Church. Lay members of synods and assemblies no more 'represent' their constituencies in terms of background, views and commitment than do Trade Union and other elites represent their rank and file. The laity in the General Synod of the Church of England perforce have jobs which make daytime attendance possible and are drawn from middle-class occupations even more heavily than are Anglican parishioners in general. With some notable exceptions they are also a good deal more articulate and better informed than their constituents, and probably more so than the clergy members. We can easily forget that the 'person in the pew' is not at all like this.

The views of the more articulate and committed representatives do not generalise to the laity in general. This is not to say that on some issues the ordinary laity are not *more* radical than their representatives – favourable views on the ordination of women to the priesthood are known empirically to be very widely held, but then who but the traditionalist would view women's access to such a position as 'radical'?

Some years ago I argued that the clergy gave a sort of highlighted exaggerated version of the fate of the Church in general, without in any way underestimating the differences between the clergy and laity. I emphasised that clergy differed on two critical factors, described as

radical *vs* traditional? (in theology and ecclesiology, but also in how they approached the use of the bible and tradition), and

puritan *vs* anti-puritan

(By 'puritan' I meant a person highly committed to religion as conventionally understood within the confines of the ecclesiastical world, and by 'anti-puritan' a person whose beliefs and religious commitment is more flexibly organised in more secular culture and institutions.) Each type gave rise not only to a distinct ethos ("that word which falls with a dull thud at the threshold of the mind", as Tawney nicely puts it), which is easily recognisable at theological colleges, but also gives rise to quite distinct ways of viewing what the Church and Christian commitment is and ought to be.

Paradoxically again, the radical anti-puritans, who so typified the 1960s, virtually dug their own grave, since they were in no way committed to the Church as an organisation, and it was therefore left largely to the traditional puritan who *was* thus committed to staff parishes and latterly even theological colleges. Hence, I argued, in the short run it will be the conservative suburban parishes which will flourish; and so it is. The point I failed to stress was that institutional religion has remarkably persistent and potent ways of colluding across the lay – ordained divide. It isn't simply that conservative clergy minister to conservative laity – though this is true. Rather, institutional modes of interpreting clerical authority often involve treating laity in a truly infantile way – expecting and even demanding an uncritical loyalty, humility and commitment (not, of course, to themselves *per se*, but to wider causes such as 'the Catholic faith', 'biblical Christianity' – but usually as interpreted by the clergy). Too often the laity themselves are happy to be served such secure certainties, and the fact that the elements of biblical and theological criticism have not percolated to most congregations cannot simply be due to the unwillingness of clergy to pass on their knowledge.

Nonetheless, clerical protectiveness of the simple sensibilities of their flocks is an all too potent mixture when combined with a lay resistance to teaching which may threaten life outside the narrow confines of 'the religious'. In many ways the incidents associated with the fire at York Minster at the consecration of the Bishop of Durham typify the infantilism of some clergy, who were the most vocal supporters of the 'judgement theory'. It would have been instructive to ask the same clergy of what blasphemy or theological unorthodoxy the peasants of Colombia were guilty when the Almighty responded yet more unequivocally by volcanic action.

The radical questioning of the 1960s was often equally one-sided; it largely failed to generate a spirituality to which its adherents could relate and which could have deepened their criticism and it was, by and large, uninterested in the institutional arrangements necessary to sustain their approach. To that extent it deserved to fail, and it is not surprising that it did not produce a second generation, for it did not seem to want one.

Some critics upbraided me at the time for encouraging a sort of radical death-wish for the established Church by articulating a prophecy which could become self-fulfilling. This is a misinterpretation of what I did suggest. First, the prediction I made seemed to me to be sociologically realistic, whether or not I approved of it. But there is more to it than that. To explain why, I need to become more speculative, and it may give the prediction some life if the issues are now illustrated both by what seems to be happening, and by what seems virtually excluded from happening.

First, there can be no return to the universal, traditional, central role of "the Church" (as Niebuhr saw in the United States, identifying the denomination as the stable form of organisation). In this sense, secularisation has caught up. Certainly, Eastern Orthodoxy and national Roman Catholic Churches such as that in Poland will continue to flourish, and even offer hope to both traditionalists and sectarians bent upon restoring the *status quo ante*. But the reasons for the persistence of such Churches has as much to do with political identity and their organisational rigidity as with the fact that they appear to offer the solace of an unchanging faith – not least to disturbed Anglicans. The only contexts where the Church is apparently growing is where it is offering *either* a radically non-authoritarian structure and theology (as in Latin America), *or* is tenaciously promulgating fundamentalist structures and theology. It should now be clear that personally I would prefer the former, largely because it does respond to all three needs of the Christian, and in a manner which respects the institutional component, without enduing it with sacred authority. In one sense it is utopian to expect the Church to take seriously what Jesus said when washing the disciples' feet and in the dispute about greatness, and it is one of the most persistent imperatives in the gospel which is blithely ignored at an organisational level in all types of Church polity. But it is also the starting point for re-thinking suitable organisational structures.

What, then, of the reasons for remaining in the Church? We cannot fully justify this, I think, in terms of the categories, processes or needs I have mentioned as ways of resolving the paradox between gospel demands and institutional imperatives. To do this one must begin with the radical disjunction between the Kingdom and the Church. By the Kingdom I mean the core of the demands and life required by Jesus in the gospel accounts, as interpreted with the benefit of theological and historical competence, and I of course recognise that the gospel and other biblical records are themselves the product of the worshipping Church. That is not at issue. But there is a distinction to be made between the gospel demands and the institutional organisation(s) claiming to represent these demands – and much else. Both are necessary sociologically; you cannot live in the Kingdom in an organisational vacuum, but neither can the institutional structure, however well-intentioned, demand equivalence with the Kingdom. The two will normally be in tension and precarious balance, tipped when a radical insight or renewal breaks through or requires alternative institutional arrangements.

I take it as axiomatic that the Christian's unconditional commitment is to the Kingdom, even though there may well be allegiance to the Church, and where they conflict there can be no doubt of the Kingdom's priority. To accept this involves the virtual abandonment of imagery which equates the two (the heavenly Jerusalem, the body of Christ and the familiar phrases from hymnody). There should also be a recognition that so long as the priority of the Kingdom is secure, the Church (rightly now the pilgrim Church) may reasonably make claims to speak in the name of and with the authority of Christ. But since it (she?) is under the judgement of the Kingdom, the institutional arrangements of the Church must be part of that judgement. Not surprisingly, Christians whose secondary allegiance is to the Church are not going to take seriously such organisational strictures as the forbidding of intercommunion. But equally, the Church is going to be understandably anxious to ensure that its authority is recognised and kept to, even if in its heart of hearts it knows that discipline or mode of securing obedience is not justifiable in terms of the Christian allegiance.

The people of God become then not the silly sheep governed by a divinely-selected leadership, but – as put recently by a Jesuit priest – "bewildered, confused or disillusioned Christians, who have a love-hate relationship with the Church to which they belong or belonged." On my argument, that love-hate relationship is neither accidental nor unfortunate, but should be the normal and expected way in which we respond to ecclesiastical claims.

It would be easy to make this sound like a new Protestantism or simply a utopian demand, and it is therefore important to stress that it is written within the Catholic tradition and by one who has often found more of the Kingdom in the Church of Rome than elsewhere.

But I am not so naive as to believe that what I think the Church can be, and indeed ought to be, is actually what it is likely to be. Internal currents make it far more likely that a polarisation will occur between organised traditionalists of all varieties and churchmanships, and the rest. Fortunately, such re-alignment across denominational barriers also occurs in the non-traditionalist area, where Hans Küng above all has shown how a sociologically informed theology can help in reconstruction and in the important task of setting the agenda for the Church's role, away from concentration on ecclesiastical problems of genuine, if of lowly, importance and towards its involvement in redeeming the whole of man — individuals, structures and all.

A Shilling for Candles

Josephine Tey is one of the best known and best loved of all crime writers. She began to write full-time after the successful publication of her first novel, *The Man in the Queue* (1929), which introduced Inspector Grant of Scotland Yard. In 1937 she returned to crime writing with *A Shilling for Candles*, but it wasn't until after the Second World War that the majority of her crime novels were published. Josephine Tey died in 1952, leaving her entire estate to the National Trust.

Praise for Josephine Tey

'A detective story with a very considerable difference. Ingenious, stimulating and very enjoyable' *Sunday Times*

'One of the best mysteries of all time' *New York Times*

'As interesting and enjoyable a book as they will meet in a month of Sundays' *Observer*

'First-rate mystery, ably plotted and beautifully written' *Los Angeles Times*

'Suspense is achieved by unexpected twists and extremely competent storytelling . . . credible and convincing' *Spectator*

'Really first class . . . a continual delight' *Times Literary Supplement*

'Josephine Tey enjoys a category to herself, as a virtuoso in the curious . . . the nature of the deception on this occasion is too good to give away' *New Statesman*

'Tey's style and her knack for creating bizarre characters are among the best in the field' *New Yorker*

4 5 0046678 0

Published by Arrow Books 2011

11

Copyright © The National Trust 1953

In accordance with the late Josephine Tey's wish, all author's profits from this book
will go to the National Trust for Places of Historic Interest or Natural Beauty

The right of Josephine Tey to be identified as the author of this work has been
asserted with the Copyright, Designs and Patents Act, 1988

First published in Great Britain in 1953 by William Heinemann

Arrow Books
Random House, 20 Vauxhall Bridge Road
London SW1V 2SA

www.randomhouse.co.uk

Addresses for companies within The Random House Group Limited can be found at:
www.randomhouse.co.uk/offices.htm

The Random House Group Limited Reg. No. 954009

A CIP catalogue record for this book
is available from the British Library

ISBN 9780099556688

Penguin Random House is committed to a sustainable future for
our business, our readers and our planet. This book is made from
Forest Stewardship Council® certified paper.

MIX
Paper from
responsible sources
FSC® C018179

inted and bound in Great Britain by Clays Ltd, Elcograf S.p.A.